Multimodal Sentiment Analysis Using Deep Learning and Metaheuristic Optimization

Dawn Fover

Content

List of Figures

List of Tables

Chapter 1

Introduction

In the era of digital communication and the rapid expansion of internet access, people are increasingly sharing information, expressing opinions and engaging with others on various platforms. The Internet has become a worldwide personalization platform and has brought billions of people together by using desktops, tablets and smartphones. The effect of this change has led to the development of a data-driven culture, which is characterized by the real active participation of users who contribute content in various forms of online media. The emerging trend of internet services has led to an abundance of user-generated content, including comments, reviews and posts such as social networks, e-commerce, food delivery and travel booking services. This kind of online content not only affects the buying patterns of consumers, but also transforms the manner in which companies obtain consumer feedback and use it to advance their products and services.

The rise of user-generated content is probably one of the most well-known examples through the digital transformation. There are different types of user content, appearing in the form of text, images, or video, the common characteristic is that it is voluntarily created and publicly shared by individual users rather than professional authors, companies, or media outlets. These contents are generally informal, spontaneous and deeply personal in nature, that is, an honest showcase of user experiences. This differs from mainstream media, which go through some filters and editing; in other words, user-generated content conveys unaltered ideas and emotions from individuals themselves, thus highly useful in understanding public opinion, trending topics and common social choices. It is rapidly growing on various review websites and social media platforms [1].

1.1 Importance of Reviews

A review is a statement that a user shares to express their thoughts or opinions about a product, service, event, or experience. It can be as simple as a single score or as long as a full story. They can also have images or videos in them [2]. The growing number of people writing reviews has created a database of data that is constantly changing and growing and full of sentiments. These reviews can provide researchers with a lot of data to work with when looking at behavior and opinions.

User reviews are essential in making consumer choices and affecting the reputation of the company. They provide direct insights into consumer experiences, preferences and expectations; therefore, they have become a useful source of feedback for companies. Reviews not only help potential customers make educated decisions, but also direct businesses to improve their offerings, services and approaches to customer participation [3]. Recent industry studies indicate that more than 95% of buyers check online reviews before buying, and almost 80% of customers believe these reviews as much as personal referrals. This includes instances such as Amazon customer reviews, TripAdvisor travel stories, YouTube video reviews, Instagram image-based reviews and Google Maps or Zomato user ratings [4]. There are two main types of user reviews: quantitative and qualitative. Each category gives a different kind of information about sentiments.

1.1.1 Quantitative Reviews

These are organized numerical ratings that are often shown as star ratings (e.g., 1-5 stars), percentage scores (e.g. 85%), or Likert scales (e.g., strongly agree to strongly disagree). It is easy to combine and analyze quantitative reviews using statistical and rule-based methods. This makes it easy to quickly figure out how people feel about many things, such as the average satisfaction score or the overall product rating, but do not have enough context to be useful. A 3-star rating does not say whether the user did not like the product's quality, customer service, or price [5].

1.1.2 Qualitative Reviews

These reviews contain free-form text, images uploaded by users, video testimonials and spoken audio feedback. Qualitative reviews are unstructured and mostly descriptive; hence, they reveal the circumstances behind the user's sentiments. For example, a text review that says "The food was great, but the service was very slow," expresses mixed feelings that are absent from a rating of a number. In a video, facial expressions, the tone of voice in an audio clip, or visual signals in an image can also convey how someone feels. Qualitative reviews are harder to assess because they do not have a clear structure and require advanced techniques such as Natural Language Processing (NLP), Computer Vision (CV) and multimodal fusion to do this [6,7].

Analyzing these reviews becomes important, as it supports applications such as brand reputation monitoring, product development, personalized recommendations and predictive modeling of market trends. Sentiment Analysis (SA) serves as a tool for understanding human sentiments, opinions and ideas from these diverse data streams.

1.2 Sentiment Analysis

SA, also known as opinion mining, is a specialized area within Artificial Intelligence (AI) that falls under the broader domain of NLP, deals with the phenomena of finding, extracting and categorizing emotions, opinions or other subjective data across any kind of data and most frequently referring to text-based data, as well as images, audio, or video. The main objective is to identify the sentiment polarity (positive, negative, or neutral) used in the content, and, in a more complex case, to analyze certain emotions such as joy, anger, or sadness [8]. It requires a number of computational steps, such as data pre-processing, feature extraction and Machine Learning (ML), Deep Learning (DL) and lexicon-based classification. SA, originally used for text-based analysis, has evolved into multimodal analysis, incorporating speech, facial expressions and visual context. It is crucial in customer feedback, brand analysis and social media analytics. Computational models are developed for various types of data to capture the feelings effectively.

Text-based SA is a computational process used to process sentiments and attitudes in textual data. It involves various approaches, including lexicon-based, ML-based, hybrid and DL-based methods. Lexicon-based approaches use a pre-existing sentiment dictionary, while ML-based approaches use supervised learning types like Decision Trees (DT), Naive Bayes (NB), Support Vector Machines (SVM) and Logistic Regression (LR) to categorize text and predict polarity. DL-based SA models learn features from data, using Convolutional Neural Networks (CNNs) for spatial patterns and Recurrent Neural Networks (RNNs) for sequential data. Transformer-based models use self-attention for deep contextual relationships, while aspect-based sentiment analysis detects sentiment associated with specific aspects. Transfer learning fine-tunes pre-trained models for domain-specific tasks [9].

Beyond text, visual information is crucial to convey human feelings, especially in social media applications. Visual SA uses features like facial expressions, body movements and aesthetics to understand emotions. CV methods interpret these cues, using CNNs and DL models. Visual SA is used in emotional AI, user experience and social media analytics, often overlooked by text-only methods [10].

One other emerging area is speech SA, which is based on audio signals, addressing issues with accent, pitch, pace, language and sentence structure. Using Mel-frequency cepstral coefficients (MFCCs), pitch, energy and tone, sentiment identification is done using Hidden Markov Models (HMM), RNN, or CNNs. This emerging area helps discover implicit and explicit messages in verbal communication. Furthermore, the use of video SA incorporates textual, audio and visual modalities to gain a more comprehensive understanding of user sentiment. Spoken language, facial expression, gestures and dynamics of a scene are the things a video usually contains. Whether it is a vlog, a review, social media videos, or anything of that matter, they all contribute to the manner of showing emotion. The analysis is based on feature extraction of transcribed text, voice tone and facial/body movements with DL models such as CNNs, RNNs and transformer-based network structures [11].

As digital content becomes increasingly multimodal, i.e., the shared reviews are not only in the form of text but also images and videos, which provide an important and wide range of information. Research indicates that more than 90% of internet buyers write text-based feedback following a transaction. Over 60% of users, however, add images to their reviews to visually back their comments; over 25% of customers provide video reviews [12]. This trend obviously shows that modern customer feedback is instinctively multimodal, and so, it is crucial to create a system that should be able to process and analyse text, image and video-based evaluations for thorough sentiment knowledge. Conventional SA focused on text, ignoring images and videos that contain important emotive context. Also, many researchers worked on unimodal systems, i.e., only for text, images, or video. The growing complexity of human communication in the digital age has highlighted the limitations of traditional, text-only sentiment analysis systems and created a pressing need for MSA [13] .

1.3 Multimodal Sentiment Analysis

Multimodal Sentiment Analysis (MSA) means analyzing sentiment using different types of data, such as Text (T), Image (I), Audio (A) and Video

(V). In this research, these different data formats are used as input to predict sentiment. At present, MSA is an emerging research domain, and advancing efforts in this area is imperative due to the plethora of online community platforms, such as Facebook and Twitter, where individuals articulate their views through text, images, audio and video recordings. Due to the substantial volume of opinion-rich multimodal content, an effective analysis method is essential. In this instance, MSA may be bimodal, integrating any two modalities (text and images, text and video, or images and video), or trimodal, incorporating all three modalities (text, video and images). This multimedia content offers detailed knowledge on a certain issue; hence, MSA is an essential field of study.

For instance, nowadays users share reviews of a particular restaurant in various formats T, I, V. To generate a thorough and unified sentiment about that particular restaurant, there is a need to process these multimodal inputs. Textual reviews provide detailed information about the food and services; images reveal the presentation quality and ambiance; and video provides customer interactions and an overall dining experience. Instead of only considering a single modality, integrating the modalities can be essential for organizations aiming to enhance customer happiness and optimize their services. A few instances may be such that while text reviews look mostly positive, images or videos sometimes exhibit negative or neutral sentiments. Focusing on text only in such a case would lead to misinterpretation as to what the real user experience was. Hence, integration of multiple modalities becomes critical for correct sentiment classification and understanding it better in terms of the actual user's opinion. A variety of fusion techniques in MSA are employed to integrate comprehensive information from different modalities, including T, I and V. Early fusion corresponds to the merging of features at the input stage. Late fusion occurs when output scores from classifiers of different modalities are combined. Hybrid fusion is an agglomeration of early and late fusion techniques for a possibly improved performance. Temporal fusion aligns data with respect to time, useful when dealing with video analysis. Utterance-level fusion and word-level fusion consider fusion of modalities at utterance and word levels, respectively, for fine-level sentiment detection. Sequence-to-sequence fusion exploits sequence modeling to handle temporal dependencies and quantum-based fusion adds a new flavor from quantum theory to account for complex interactions between modalities. The goal of these methods is to better and deeply analyze sentiments through effective combination of multimodal data [14, 15].

Recently, tremendous studies have been made in the field of MSA because of the exponential increase in user content in various formats, including T, I, A and V. The majority of existing models are limited to only working with single modalities (unimodal), normally text, or on bimodal combinations such as text and image or text and audio, with limited work exploring fully integrated trimodal systems that effectively combine text, image and video or audio inputs [16]. Most current solutions use basic methods, like combining features from each type of input into one single feature vector for classification. Other methods utilized the modalities separately and integrated them into single predictions with late fusion approaches, e.g., averaging or majority voting. Additionally, existing research does not consider the combined use of multimodal user reviews that are available on real world platforms such as Amazon, TripAdvisor, or

YouTube. On these sites, people tend to express their thoughts through a text, images (like product images and ambiance) and videos (including vlogs, unboxings and reactions). Nevertheless, these platforms lack a common system that can effectively process these diverse inputs and generate a consolidated sentiment score or rating. Current models are also limited in their domain-specific generalizability since most of the training data is small or selected so as not to represent the complexity of real-time social media content [17] . These difficulties also reaffirm the necessity to have more flexible, adaptive and optimized MSA structures that could not only handle multiple and incomplete multimodal data but also do so with a high level of accuracy in the classification of sentiments [18].

MSA has gained significant relevance across various domains due to its ability to interpret sentiments expressed through multiple forms of user-generated content, such as text, images and videos. In e-commerce, it helps companies understand customer preferences and experiences by analyzing product reviews that include written feedback, images of products and unboxing videos, thereby improving recommendations and customer satisfaction. In social media analytics, this approach plays a vital role in monitoring public opinion, brand perception, and trending sentiments by processing diverse content formats on platforms like Twitter, Instagram and YouTube. It is also widely used in entertainment and media, where user reactions to movies, advertisements and events are evaluated-based on multimodal posts. In the healthcare sector, it contributes to mental health monitoring by analysing patients' verbal expressions, facial cues and emotional tone in therapy sessions or online interactions. Furthermore, in politics and public policy, it helps researchers and governments gauge public sentiment on policy decisions and political events using posts that combine speech, visuals and commentary. These applications highlight the importance of MSA in delivering richer, more accurate sentiment understanding from complex, real-world data.

1.4 Motivation

- Due to the development of social networks, there is a rise in the posting of reviews across multiple content formats, with images and videos, as people find it exceptionally simple to communicate feelings.
- Traditional SA methods have mainly focused on unimodality, that is, considering only one modality at a time, which is not applicable in the current situation, as the internet is fueled with multimodal content data, which can include images, videos, or combinations of different modalities. Therefore, performing SA on such data is a very crucial task. Hence, a need to explore MSA is needed.
- The system can be used for the analysis of various forms of user-generated content, such as social media, customer reviews and multimedia content, making it highly valuable and impactful in real-world applications.

1.5 General Objectives

- To build a comprehensive sentiment analysis system that can process reviews in various formats such as text, images and videos.

- To enhance the accuracy and reliability of sentiment detection by using advanced deep learning models tailored to each modality.
- To develop a unified method for combining information from multiple input types using a dynamic and adaptive fusion approach.
- To improve feature selection and reduce complexity through optimization techniques for better model performance.
- To ensure that the model works effectively in real-world applications, such as customer feedback analysis in sectors such as e-commerce, restaurants and tourism.
- To validate the system's performance through comparative experiments using standard sentiment datasets and evaluation metrics.

To understand the foundation of existing sentiment analysis systems and to highlight the research gaps addressed in this study, it is important to review past developments in the field. The following section provides an analytical overview of previous work, focusing on sentiment analysis techniques applied to different modalities such as text, images, videos and multimodal fusion. This review helps to identify the computational methods that have been developed, their strengths and limitations, and sets the rationale for the proposed model.

1.6 Organization of Thesis

After the Abstract, the rest of the report is organized into chapters.

- Chapter 1 is the introduction, which contains sections such as an overview of the project, motivation of the project, contributions and the organization of the project.

- Chapter 2 provides a comprehensive review of the literature on existing work related to SA using text, image and video modalities. It explores the limitations in respective unimodal SA systems and tries to improve the systems. Also, it emphasizes the need for an integrated approach. The chapter concludes with an identification of the research gaps that laid the foundation for the proposed work.

- Chapter 3 focuses on contribution 1- BERT-iBiLSTM for improved feature extraction for text sentiment analysis. It involves steps such as preprocessing the text, extracting important features with Bidirectional Encoder Representations from Transformers (BERT) and an improved Bidirectional Long-Short-Term Memory (BiLSTM), choosing the best features with Dual Moth Flame Optimization (DMFO) and classifying sentiment using an ensemble model consisting of several machine learning algorithms as base classifiers. The chapter concludes with a comprehensive analysis of the experimental results, evaluated using standard performance metrics.

- Chapter 4 focuses on contribution 2- A comprehensive framework for SA of images using WaveNet-CNN for feature extraction and DMFO for feature selection. It involves preprocessing methods, feature extraction from the spatial domain and the frequency domain using custom CNN and optimal wavelet transform and optimal feature selection through DMFO and sentiment classification through the ensemble mechanism. The chapter concludes with a comprehensive analysis of the experimental results, evaluated using standard performance metrics.

- Chapter 5 focuses on contribution 3- A Hierarchical Attention-based Fusion Model (HABF) for video sentiment analysis. It describes a video SA pipeline that extracts and integrates features from visual frames, audio signals and transcribed text. These features are fused by an early fusion method using a novel hierarchical-based attention mechanism and then these fused features are classified by an ensemble model. The chapter concludes with a comprehensive analysis of the experimental results, evaluated using standard performance metrics.

- Chapter 6 focuses on contribution 4 – An integrated sentiment analysis model using multimodal inputs (text, image and video) that discusses the architecture and functionality of the model capable of processing each modality individually through respective unimodal pipelines to generate a single sentiment prediction through the late fusion mechanism in the case of multiple modalities. Hence, the model is adaptable and applicable for different input scenarios in practice, such as restaurant reviews.

- Chapter 7 focuses on the research plan for the conclusion and future work. It reflects on potential improvements to the proposed model, new directions in research that are open and opportunities to extend the work to broader application areas. Before this, the chapter summarizes the key findings, followed by an exploration of areas that deserve further investigation.

- References

Chapter 2

Literature Survey

With the rapid growth of user-generated content on current and emerging social media platforms, individuals are no longer limited to expressing their opinions solely through text. Instead, users now frequently share content in multiple formats, such as images, videos and combinations of these along with text, attaching some image or video. This shift has led to a dramatic increase in multimodal content available online, significantly enriching potential data sources for SA. Consequently, MSA has emerged as a vital area of research, offering a more holistic understanding of user sentiments compared to traditional unimodal approaches.

This section begins with a discussion of how the early systems relied predominantly on unimodal input, text, image, or video, highlighting their individual strengths and limitations and then on the integration of text and visual cues. Following this, the literature survey delves into the growing adoption of optimization algorithms for effective feature selection in text and image systems. It also explores advanced fusion strategies, challenges in aligning heterogeneous modalities and recent breakthroughs in hierarchical and context-aware fusion models that aim to improve the accuracy of sentiment prediction in real-world settings.

2.1 Evolution of Sentiment Analysis with Shift in Input Modalities

In recent years, the exponential growth of user-generated content across digital platforms has significantly transformed the landscape of SA [19]. Initially, the research in SA was focused mainly on analyzing textual data, such as product reviews, tweets and comments [20]. However, with the proliferation of image-rich platforms like Instagram and Pinterest, SA evolved to include visual content as a primary modality. The next leap came with the surge in video content on platforms such as YouTube, TikTok and Instagram reels, where users now express sentiments through facial expressions, tone of voice and dynamic visual cues, often accompanied by captions or speech transcripts. Earlier studies largely dealt with text-based sentiment analysis as put forth in . Later studies considered visuals, trying to classify sentiments based on images [21, 22].

The need for advanced sentiment understanding propelled multimodal approaches further. [23] attempted to combine text, audio and visual information from videos, while [24] advanced further to combine text, image and audio channels in another effort to predict feelings. The latest work, such as [25] and [26], emphasizes bimodal combinations mainly between text and image, reflecting changing interests in combining multiple data sources to improve the accuracy and interpretability of sentiment analysis. Few research papers discussed illustrate the evolution of input modalities in SA, from unimodal to multimodal inputs. The shift from modalities from text and images to video is observed. And now users are also using text+image as input, reflecting the growing richness of content shared online. It is observed that there is no such system that can handle unimodal and multimodal types of data.

2.2 Sentiment Analysis Systems

This section presents a comprehensive overview of existing approaches in the domain of sentiment analysis, focusing on systems developed to process textual, visual (image-based) and video-based data. As user-generated content continues to diversify across multiple formats, researchers have proposed a wide range of models tailored to different input types, each designed to interpret and classify human sentiment from specific modalities. The purpose of this review is to examine how previous studies have addressed sentiment detection within these individual modalities, highlighting the methodologies, strengths and limitations of each. Understanding the evolution of these unimodal systems lays the foundation for developing more flexible and integrated models capable of handling multimodal input in real-world scenarios.

2.2.1 Text Sentiment Analysis

This section presents an overview of the existing approaches used for analyzing sentiment in textual data. It focuses on the application of ML and DL techniques to classify opinions and emotions expressed in various forms of text, including product reviews, social media posts and comments. These approaches aim to interpret the polarity and intensity of sentiment, contributing to a deeper understanding of user attitudes and public opinion.

a. Machine Learning

In order to find and extract the relevant characteristics from the tweets, Jung Y. G. et al. [27] used feature extraction. Subsequently, multinomial NB was used for SA using these features. Using tweets labeled as positive, negative, or neutral, they performed an analysis on the sentiment140 dataset. The study [28] conducted a comparison of four ML techniques for SA. The dataset used the case study of Indian Railways, which was obtained using the Twitter social media platform classified into positive, negative, or neutral labels. Experimental results showed that 89.5% accuracy was achieved by C4.5, 89% by NB, 91.5% by SVM and 90.5% by Random Forest (RF). Twitter data pertaining to US airlines for SA using an AdaBoost model is used in [29]. The text was pre-processed to remove any unnecessary info. Data mining techniques were also employed to examine the relationships between the dataset's components. The information was obtained by gathering data from Twitter and Skytrax using certain keywords associated with the top ten airlines in the US. The studies were conducted using 75% of the data for training purposes, while the remaining 25% was set aside for testing resulting in the attainment 68%. In [30], DL techniques within a DT framework is applied to carry out document-level SA. Models like CNN and Long Short-Term Memory (LSTM) networks are used to extract features from the data and to learn the data patterns. This combination aims to improve classification accuracy and assist decision-making when classifying sentiments of documents considered as a whole versus those of their separate parts.

Narang P. et al. [31] extracted high-level textual features for sentiment analysis to detect fake news. The study seeks to seize the emotional tone of news content and detect linguistic patterns indicative of deceptive or fraudulent reporting. Techniques such as TF-IDF, word embeddings and syntactic analysis are used to extract meaningful features from text. These features describe the news content and are fed into different machine learning classifiers such as SVM, RF, DT, KNN and LR for classification. The findings indicate that SA combined with textual feature extraction can significantly improve the accuracy level of fake news detection.

b. Deep Learning

Tan K. L. et al. [32] introduced a hybrid DL approach that combines sequence and transformer models, using the Robustly optimized BERT approach (RoBERTa) for meaningful embedding spaces and the LSTM model for accurate contextual meaning capture. The model outperforms advanced methods on the IMDb, Twitter US Airline Sentiment and Sentiment140 datasets, with F1-scores of 93%, 91% and 90%, respectively. Hossen M. S. et al. [33] used DL models like CNNs and LSTMs to categorize sentiment and predict future trends of hotel reviews. The research uses varying levels of detail and emotion in user feedback. The results show that DL models improve accuracy and prediction quality compared to traditional ML methods. Garg A. & Kaliyar R. K. [34] introduced PSent20, a DL model for analyzing political sentiment in real-time social media data, focusing on Twitter. The model used advanced frameworks like BERT or LSTM to analyze tweets and categorize sentiment. The study evaluates PSent20 compared to other models, highlighting its enhanced accuracy and ability to analyze real-time data, demonstrating its precision in political sentiment analysis. Jain P. K. et al. [35] presented a model that combines CNNs and

LSTMs to analyze sentiment in consumer-generated content. The CNN extracts local patterns, while the LSTM captures temporal connections. The model improves sentiment categorization accuracy compared to CNN or LSTM alone, but lacks in-depth analysis of optimization approaches and feature selection influence. Dhiman A. et al. [36] explored sentiment categorization in Hindi, a language with limited resources compared to English. Researchers used a hybrid deep learning approach, CNN for feature extraction LSTM networks for sequence modeling. Data pretreatment includes tokenization, stop-word removal and addressing inflections. The model outperforms conventional methods like SVM or NB in accurately categorizing sentiments in Hindi text. The approach is resilient even with a small dataset, making it suitable for other low-resource languages.

Salmony M. Y. et al. [37] proposed an attention mechanism in DL models for SA. The attention mechanism assigns varying weights to words or phrases in the input text, allowing the model to focus on the most relevant sections. The model architecture includes an embedding layer, LSTM or RNN layers, an attention layer and a final classification layer. The study found that the attention layer significantly improves the model's performance, especially when sentiment is influenced by specific phrases. Priya C. S. R. & Deepalakshmi P. [38] showed that hybrid models, including CNN and LSTM, significantly improve SA. Contextual embeddings like BERT show superior performance over standard embeddings like Word2Vec and GloVe in SA tasks on unstructured hotel reviews. Rhanoui M. et al. [39] presented a model that combines CNNs and BiLSTM for SA at the document level. The model extracts abstract features, focusing on local patterns, while BiLSTM analyzes the text in both forward and backward directions. This technique surpasses conventional machine learning and DL models in SA tasks. The study [40] conducted SA on movie reviews sourced from IMDb. Several preprocessing processes were undertaken to eliminate insignificant letters, symbols, redundant words and stop words. Subsequently, the CountVectorizer was employed for the purpose of feature extraction. Subsequently, the characteristics were inputted into the NB, SVM, LR, KNN, ensemble and CNN models. The CNN model's accuracy is the most effective, reaching 99.33%.

Similarly [41] proposed the ESFMS model which enhances SA by combining multimodal feature selection with an ensemble classification strategy. It maximizes feature sets from various modalities, enhancing sentiment classification precision. The model's performance is improved in feedback evaluation scenarios with diverse data sources. The study suggests exploring optimization strategies for improved feature selection and computing efficiency. Rahman et al. [42] proposed the RoBERTa-BiLSTM sentiment analysis framework that integrates the contextual representation capabilities of RoBERTa with the sequence modeling capabilities of a BiLSTM. This amalgamation improves sentiment classification to obtain the semantic context and word order. The model was tested in the IMDb, Twitter USairline and Sentiment140 datasets and scored high accuracy 92.36%, 80.74% and 82.25% on each of the datasets, respectively.

The model proposed in [43] called ABCDM is a composite of CNN and RNN bidirectional layers (LSTM and Gated Recurrent Unit (GRU)) used to extract local and contextual features of a text with the added feature of an attention mechanism to concentrate on words rich in sentiment. It has been evaluated on five Amazon review datasets and three Twitter datasets and shown state-of-the-art performance both in short and long texts. The model performed better than a few deep learning baselines having a high level of effectiveness in detecting sentiment polarity due to the fact that it can integrate convolutional, sequential and attention-based learning. The hybrid approach of CNN with the LSTM network to perform SA on the big data of social media called Co-LSTM is proposed in [44]. The local semantic patterns across the text are captured using CNN layers and the sequential format of the text using LSTM layers. The design of this architecture takes into consideration the large volume and diversity of social big data. The model was tested on domain-specific datasets such as the social media dataset and the review dataset in which the model showed better accuracy and F1 score than the traditional LSTM and CNN model. Co-LSTM also shows better performance in getting real meaningful sentiment features of noisy and unstructured user-generated content.

2.2.2 Image Sentiment Analysis

Recent years have yielded advances in image-based SA, leading to the development of various methodologies focused on evaluating emotions in content disseminated throughout social media platforms. Despite increasing popularity, these models persistently exhibit issues related to performance consistency and classification accuracy. To address these limitations, researchers have proposed many ways to improve the accuracy of sentiment analysis in visual data. This section examines these techniques, particularly their application in restaurant review analysis, food image classification and the emotional interpretation of user-generated content.

This study [47] uses the improved variant of CNN Inception-v3 and auxiliary features to improve general performance in classifying images in the dataset, including FER2013 and JAFFE. In another [48], artificial feature extraction with a Gabor filter is combined with an evolutionary algorithm to optimize SVM hyperparameters with genetic algorithms. This means that relatively high classification accuracies are achieved (94.20% on the CK dataset and 94.26% on the CK+ dataset). In a different study [49], the DCNN-based model with an underlying architecture called AlexNet is implemented to differentiate among various emotional states and the result obtained is 93.66% average accuracy of the data in the CK and CK + datasets, establishing the success of deep architectures in image sentiment classification. Moreover, the HERO model [50], as one of the CNN-based hybrid ensembles, incorporates three separate sub-networks into a unified framework to enhance the process of emotion recognition.

The work examines how two pertinent CNN hyperparameters (i.e., filter sizes and network depth) affect classification in the FER-2013 dataset. With the help of these experiments, the best combinations achieve optimization that could increase the accuracy of emotion detection. A different research [51] presents specially adapted CNN models that are best suited for visual sentiment analysis. These models focus on combining the features of a product image with the textual metadata and provide a complete comprehension of the consumer sentiment. The aim of such multimodal approaches is to provide solutions to the drawbacks of traditional text-only sentiment systems that cannot grasp the richness of the visual content.

The field of image SA continues to encounter notable challenges from existing image representation methods, ML classifiers and fusion techniques. Certain models still rely on basic representations such as pixel-level information and manually engineered features, which cannot effectively capture subtle emotional and contextual nuances within visual data, thus restricting their ability to learn high-level abstractions effectively [52, 53]. Additionally, many systems utilize conventional classifiers with fully connected layers, which, despite their general utility, lack the expressive power of DL architectures. As a result, these models often struggle to model complex interdependencies in visual sentiment tasks, leading to suboptimal performance [54–56]. Another prominent issue lies in integrating diverse visual descriptors derived from various frequency- and spatial-domain transformation methods, which often produce heterogeneous feature sets that are difficult to unify effectively. Most current solutions do not use good methods to combine these different features, greatly affecting their ability to classify accurately and reducing how well they can tell things apart [57–60].

The RA-DLNet deep model applies residual attention modeling methods to analyze emotions in images and has a deep convolutional structure in [61]. The remaining attention layers allow the model to focus on areas of the image that are rich in emotion, making it easier to interpret and more precise. The architecture was assessed on eight benchmarks with art-image and social media image sets. The results revealed that the RA-DLNets performed better than the baseline CNNs (VGG-16, VGG-19, ResNet-50, Inception-V3 and Xception), and were able to generate an accurate sentiment analysis of 89–90% in Twitter-based sentiment data. In this strategy [62], a pretrained ResNet50 is used to extract early image highlights, which are classified at that point using a gradient boost ensemble technique. The method was tested using two sets that included emotional images labeled: CrowdFlower and GAPED. The model demonstrated robust performance, achieving scores of up to 98% in GAPED and 87% on CrowdFlower, utilizing the most advanced indicators available in the field.

Table 2.1 and Table 2.2 show that the authors used methods that only considered spatial features using CNN and the lack of feature selection techniques.

Table 2.1: Summary of Image Sentiment Analysis Techniques and Limitations

Ref.	**Year**	**Algorithm Used**	**Dataset Used**	**Dataset Size**	**Feature Selection Method**	**Limitations**
[21]	2022	Deep CNN	Disaster images	3679 images	None	Limited generalization to real-world scenarios; lacks feature selection
[64]	2019	Weakly Supervised Coupled Networks	Flickr and Instagram	Not specified	None	Weak supervision results in lower accuracy in noisy real-world data
[22]	2017	CNN	Review images	96,846 images	Item and User-Oriented CNN	Higher computational cost, lacks advanced feature selection
[63]	2022	DCNN	Restaurant Review Images	Not specified	None	No feature selection; generalization issues with unstructured data
[47]	2023	Inception-V3 (Transfer Learning)	FER2013, JAFFE	FER2013: 35,887; JAFFE: 213	None	High computational cost; limited interpretability

Table 2.2: Summary of Image Sentiment Analysis Techniques and Limitations (Continued)

Ref.	Year	Algorithm Used	Dataset Used	Dataset Size	Feature Selection Method	Limitations
[49]	2021	Deep CNN	FER2013, JAFFE	FER2013: 35,887; JAFFE: 213	None	Performance depends on gradient features; sensitive to noise
[65]	2022	Gabor Filters + CNN	Custom Social Media Dataset	7800 images	None	High processing cost; scalability issues in real-time deployment
[57]	2017	Wavelet + SVM, KNN	CK+, JAFFE	FER2013: 35,887; JAFFE: 213	None	SWT alone may miss relevant features; poor large-scale performance
[58]	2024	DWT + Deep CNN	Custom Multi-Focus Dataset	40 pairs of multifocus images	None	Complex fusion; high computation; tuning required

2.2.3 Audio Sentiment Analysis

Some of the traditional methods in audio sentiment and emotion recognition include conventional ML algorithms such as SVM, multi-layer perceptions, Gaussian mixture models, NB and Hidden Markov Model (HMM) [67, 68] performed SVM classification on well-known benchmark datasets EMO-VO, Urdu speech samples, eNTERFACE, RAVDESS, SAVEE and EMO-DB. while extracting speech features such as Mel Frequency Magnitude Coefficients, MFCCs, log-frequency power coefficients and linear prediction cepstral coefficients. However, with the emergence of DL, methods such as Artificial Neural Network (ANN),Deep neural networks, CNN, RNN, GRU, LSTM, BiLSTM and Bi-GRU have been increasingly employed for audio-based sentiment representation learning to improve classification performance [69, 70]. Similar was the work of [71], that proposed a neural architecture taking as inputs mean values of a 60 audio features, comprising 20 MFCCs, 20 first-order delta coefficients and 20 second-order delta-delta coefficients fed into an ANN and achieved 82.3% and 87.8% accuracies on RAVDESS and EMO-DB, respectively.

Praseetha V. M. & Jobby P. P [72] developed a GRU-based model with filter-bank energy features extracted from speech signals, which attained a remarkable accuracy of 93% on the augmented TESS dataset. [73], on the other hand, developed a hybrid CNN–LSTM architecture and tested it across multiple emotional speech corpora, including CREMA, SAVEE, TESS and RAVDESS. They used a feature set consisting of MFCCs, Zero Crossing Rate (ZCR) and Root Mean Square (RMS) energy and found that it worked well across varied classes of emotion.

2.2.4 Video Sentiment Analysis

The rise of modern social media platforms has empowered users to share their personal experiences and emotions through videos on a wide range of topics. Videos are inherently multimodal, as they simultaneously incorporate visual elements, spoken audio and embedded text, making them a rich source of sentiment cues. This section explores recent research efforts focused on fusion techniques across these modalities and highlights the progress, challenges and future directions in developing effective video SA systems.

An interactive framework to further improve sentiment classification [74] based on a quantum-inspired approach has been proposed to model the interactive dynamics that exist between the various modalities. Although this method leads to an increase in classification accuracy, it also has the problem of high computational complexity as well as not being able to scale up easily when using large datasets. The framework assesses performance in terms of the CMU-MOSEI and CMU-MOSI datasets, which both consist of labeled videos and contain text-synchronized audio and video data. Moreover, the joint chained interactive attention model [75] is also designed to enhance cross-modal alignment, however, by considering the per-modality-specific dependencies. To draw the features, the model relies on BiLSTM in the text segment, Librosa in the audio segment, ResNet in the visual segment and the CMU-MOSEI dataset in verification. The other model [76] uses a transformer-based way of extracting text features, while audio and visual feature extraction is done using Librosa and CNN, respectively. The transformer gives precedence to the textual features, and in this case other modalities are aligned to them. Despite the good results of such an approach on text-based sentiment tasks, this approach has drawbacks due to the inability to properly capture the emotions portrayed by non-verbal cues, e.g., in slight facial expressions or inflections in tone that may often not be explicitly described in the text version of the data.

In the study [77], the researchers used custom sentiment datasets based on aspect-based sentiment derived from CMU-MOSEI and other resources to explore improved feature extraction and fusion strategies. The focus lies on achieving precise segment-level alignment between text and audio, along with fine-grained alignment of visual modality-specific features. This technique improves sentiment prediction accuracy, particularly when analyzing lengthy and feature-rich reviews. In another approach, [78] proposed an innovative fusion mechanism that learns shared and unique modality-specific representations. This design significantly improves the model's ability to generalize while demonstrating robustness to noise and missing data. Using the CMU-MOSEI dataset, they dynamically process text with BiLSTM and extract visual features through ResNet. Meanwhile, the study [79] incorporates text embeddings, audio and visual cues from the CMU-MOSEI and CMU-MOSI datasets. It combines multiple techniques with an emphasis on aspect relevance for sentiment classification. The model achieves strong results across standard benchmarks, effectively handling modality overlap and noise, while showcasing its practical robustness in real-world multimodal sentiment tasks. Tables 2.3 and 2.4 provide a summary of MSA models and fusion techniques.

Table 2.3: Summary of MSA Models and Fusion Techniques

Ref.	**Year**	**Methods Used**	**Fusion Techniques**	**Dataset**	**Dataset Size**	**Accu (%)**	**Limitations**
[80]	2025	Bayesian modeling, uncertainty quantification	Probabilistic fusion	CMU-MOSI	93 videos	82.30	Trade-off between accuracy and confidence; complex calibration
[81]	2025	Attribute-level correlation learning	Attribute-level correlation fusion	CMU-MOSI	93 videos	82.20	Ignores hierarchical dependencies; modality imbalance issues
[82]	2025	Knowledge injection + ambiguity modeling	Late fusion + attention-guided fusion	CMU-MOSI, CH-SIMS	93 videos; 2,281 clips	82.13	Relies on external knowledge; performance degrades with missing modalities

Table 2.4: Summary of MSA Models and Fusion Techniques (Continued)

Ref.	Year	Methods Used	Fusion Techniques	Dataset	Dataset Size	Acc (%)	Limitations
[83]	2025	Decomposition network; unimodal label learning	Intermediate fusion	CMU-MOSI, CMU-MOSEI	93 (MOSI); 3228 (MOSEI) videos	81.40	Requires additional label generation; complex training pipeline
[84]	2025	Attention mechanism; GRU	Multi-level attention fusion	CMU-MOSI, CMU-MOSEI	93 (MOSI); 3228 (MOSEI) videos	81.80 (CMU-MOSI)	Does not model uncertainty; sensitive to noisy modalities
[85]	2022	Topic modeling; MFCC and energy features; frame-level CNN	Early fusion	Custom product review videos; CMU-MOSI	93 videos (MOSI); custom size not reported	81.50	Limited scalability; weak inter-modal dependency modeling
[86]	2020	GRU	Early fusion	CMU-MOSI, CMU-MOSEI	93 (MOSI); 3228 (MOSEI) videos	81.19	Struggles with long conversations and multimodal conflicts
[87]	2021	BiLSTM	Early fusion	CMU-MOSI	93 videos	80.18	Lacks robust optimization; limited scalability
[88]	2016	Topic modeling (text); spectral audio features; frame-based visual features	Early fusion	POM (Persuasion Opinion Multimedia) dataset	1000 videos	70.85	Focused on persuasiveness rather than comprehensive sentiment modeling
[80]	2015	CNN	Late fusion	Twitter image dataset (TTI, TTD)	Not specified	79.00	Considers only visual modality; ignores text and audio

2.2.5 Text and Visual Sentiment Analysis

This subsection explores text and visual sentiment analysis, a bimodal approach in which textual data is analyzed alongside visual content. Combining these two modalities allows for richer sentiment interpretation than using either alone. This bimodal integration serves as a foundational step toward more advanced MSA systems that aim to capture the full spectrum of user expression.

K. Zhang et al. [90] proposed an unsupervised maximum mean discrepancy, which uses the cross-modal approach to transfer learning that works between images and textual content and uses LSTM to classify sentiment polarity. For image feature extraction, it uses VGGNet-16 and for text(captions) uses GloVe achieving an accuracy of 80%. The limitations identified are that the audio-video modality can also be considered to improve accuracy and that the model should be optimized. In order to address the issues of unexplainable hash codes, shallow models and immutable direct projection in an integrated model to support large-scale multimedia retrieval using image and text as input, [91] proposed a SIDMH method that generates hash codes taking into account both the nearest neighbor similarity and semantic similarity inside a deep hashing architecture. For feature extraction of image, CNN and for text, BoW was used.

For multimodal emotion analysis, [92] proposed the multi-view attentional network, which obtains the semantic features of image-text for a self-created image-text dataset (TumEmo) based on emotion. The null character is used to replace the content of the hashtag and punctuation such as brackets, periods and commas with the text pre-processing URL, @username. For image feature extraction, the VGG-Place and VGG-Object networks are employed to capture scene and object features, respectively, while for text, CNN and BiLSTM are utilized to extract local and long-term dependencies. This approach achieves an accuracy of approximately 72%. The author can consider scene-guided objects and object-guided scenes to increase further accuracy. F.Huang et al. [93] proposed an attention-based modality-gated LSTM which considers the word-related visual feature and for extraction of feature deep pre-trained CNN and word embeddings are used for image and text, respectively, achieving an accuracy of about 79-89%. Different fusion methods were explored to further increase the accuracy. In order to align the images with the associated text, [94] suggested a multimodal layout-driven attention network that uses distance-based coefficients to extract image positions. A featured CNN is used for image extraction and word vectors for text extraction. Thus, existing SA systems provide a solid research gap identification framework, with clear gaps in the integration of various modalities, thus motivating the inception of a general-purpose SA framework such as the one proposed in this study.

2.3 Optimization Techniques used in Text and Image Sentiment Analysis for Feature Selection

Optimization methods have now become essential for improving the performance of an SA model. These methods, particularly selection methods, can reduce redundancy in feature representation to enhance generalization of the model and select features that are highly relevant for improving classification accuracy from high-dimensional data. This section elaborates on the optimization methods used in both text and image SA to obtain more efficient and accurate results.

Illahi I. R. & Setiawan E. B. [95] proposed the model by combining FastText, RNN and Genetic Algorithm (GA). RNNs process the sequence text, while GA evaluates feature subsets, performs mutation and crossover over these subsets and then selects the best subset based on the fitness score. The experiment dataset is prepared by preprocessing social media data, such as Twitter posts or Facebook logs. After integrating the three models, FastText, RNN and GA showed that the sentiment classification rate for NB can reach 85.7% on a Twitter sentiment dataset. However, fine tuning is still required because of a number of issues related to computational complexity and GA parameters for smoother operation. Nurcahyawati V. & Mustaffa Z. [96] concentrated on the categorization using Particle Swarm Optimization (PSO) for SA. It is based on the co-operative behavior of fish and birds, with each "particle" representing a possible solution. The study used a tokenized SA dataset that underwent preprocessing, training and testing. It revealed a basal improvement in the classification rate; for sentiment, the categories moved from 75% with all the features to 85%.

Gupta D. et al. [97] introduced an adapted iteration of the Moth Flame Optimization (MFO) algorithm for selecting features in the development of a software usability model. The revised algorithm seeks to improve the efficiency and efficacy of feature selection. Aljebreen M. et al. [98] investigated the utilization of MFO in combination with hybrid DL models for sentiment classification on Twitter data, with a specific focus on sentiments related to ChatGPT. This work presents a sentiment-analysis framework that employs the skip-gram for effective feature extraction and the LSTM for capturing long-term dependencies in textual data. To further enhance its learning capacity, the model uses adaptive particle swarm optimization algorithm to adjust the weight parameters of LSTM. The model under consideration is tested on four benchmark datasets, wherein it outperforms common methods such as the LSTM, ANN and SVM. The results prove that the proposed framework captures semantic and contextual patterns appropriately, which translates into better sentiment classification accuracy. For image, authors are utilizing nature-inspired algorithms to boost the performance of visual analysis systems. These algorithms are utilized for the purpose of feature extraction from images, in an effort to identify a subset of pertinent characteristics that contribute to more accurate picture classification or analysis [99, 100].

In the literature survey, the trend in sentiment analysis methods on various modalities, including text, image, audio and video, is illuminated. The first step involved textual SA carried out mainly by ML and DL algorithms, including SVM, NB, LSTM and BERT-based models. With the growth of user-generated content to involve rich media, studies started to examine visual sentiment analysis, with CNNs, hybrid deep models and transform-based methods being used to detect emotions in images. Video SA, on the other hand, also appeared where text data, audio data and image were merged more commonly with BiLSTM, CNNs, ResNet and transformers. The development of MSA was based on the idea of utilizing two (or more) modalities and enhancing classification. Nevertheless, current systems are usually subjected to issues like poor fusion schemes, usage of only single-modality models, or the failure to dynamically cope with differing mixes of input formats. This inspires the desire to have a more flexible, coherent and strong SA system that can work on unimodal and multimodal data.

2.4 Research Gaps

Although significant progress has been made in sentiment analysis, existing approaches still face notable limitations in handling complex multimodal data. To address these issues and establish the novelty of this work, the following research gaps are identified.

- Most of the systems are limited to the unimodal modality.
- Text sentiment analysis models face limitations, such as inadequate contextual understanding and poor handling of sequential dependencies.
- For image sentiment analysis, most of the existing models focus solely on spatial features, missing out on critical frequency-related information, which can be essential for sentiment detection.
- Lack of a feature selection method for both text and image systems.
- For video sentiment analysis, the use of simple fusion techniques often involves a simple concatenation of features that fails to adapt dynamically to the varying importance of each modality.
- There is a need for an integrated and versatile model that works seamlessly with unimodal and multimodal inputs.

2.5 Problem Statement

Consumers in the modern age of digital communication share their opinions and feedback on numerous Internet platforms using a variety of media types, including text, images, videos, or combinations thereof. Traditional sentiment analysis systems deal mainly with unimodal inputs. It has been observed that reliance on a single modality for interpreting results lacks enough information and becomes less reliable when it comes to comprehending the user's sentiments. As more people rely on reviews to make decisions in marketing, product development and customer service, there is a pressing need for a system that can effectively use multimodal data as input. Therefore, the aim of the thesis is to provide an integrated model that can handle not only processing unimodal inputs (T, I and V) but also combinations of those, which enables a unified sentiment output. This complementary model will evolve into a complete sentiment analysis, providing more profound consumer insight for real-world applications such as customer feedback, marketing and online reviews, aiding in sharper business strategies.

2.6 Research Objectives

The main objective of this research is to effectively deal with multimodal inputs and to achieve this, the following research objectives are identified.

- To improve text-based sentiment analysis by enhancing the process of feature extraction and incorporating a feature selection method to achieve more accurate and reliable sentiment classification.
- To achieve sentiment understanding from visual content, a framework is developed that encompasses both feature extraction and feature selection.
- To fuse modality-based features extracted from a video as input for sentiment analysis.

- Design an integrated sentiment analysis model capable of processing multimodal inputs (text, image and video) either unimodal or in combination.

To achieve this, an integrated sentiment analysis model was developed to address the limitations of unimodal methods by enhancing text analysis, incorporating structured visual sentiment analysis, and fusing features across modalities. The adaptive framework is capable of handling both unimodal and multimodal inputs, ensuring versatility and scalability. Its applicability extends to domains such as online reviews, social media, and experience evaluation. The subsequent chapter presents the BERT-iBiLSTM for improved text sentiment analysis.

Chapter 3

Contribution 1: BERT-iBiLSTM for Improved Feature Extraction for Text Sentiment Analysis

The increasing prevalence of user-generated reviews in various formats, including text, images and videos on platforms such as e-commerce sites, hospitality portals and social media, has required the development of sentiment analysis systems capable of understanding and analyzing multimodal inputs. Traditional approaches often focus on a single modality, which can result in incomplete or biased interpretations. Figure 3.1 shows the general workflow of the proposed system that addresses each modality independently by first processing each modality through respective unimodal models for text, image and video, each optimized for extracting sentiment-specific features. The resulting sentiment scores are then combined in a late fusion stage, which dynamically adapts to the available modalities and resolves conflicting cues. This produces a prediction of unified sentiment that provides a comprehensive and reliable assessment of general sentiment for unimodal, bimodal, or multimodal inputs. Thus, in this chapter, the discussion starts with the text sentiment analysis system, whereby the design and evaluation of the unimodal model took place as the first step towards the integrated framework.

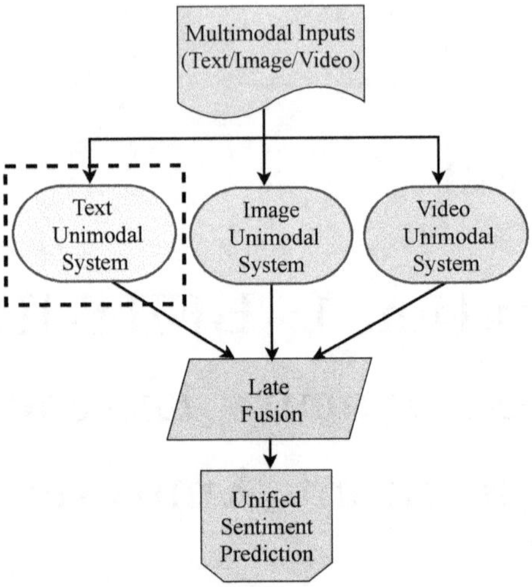

Figure 3.1: General Workflow of Proposed Integrated Model for Sentiment Analysis

Text SA plays a critical role in understanding user opinions expressed on digital platforms, especially in domains such as product reviews, social media and service feedback. Despite significant advancements, many existing systems struggle to effectively capture contextual nuances, handle long-term dependencies and filter irrelevant or redundant features. These limitations often lead to suboptimal sentiment classification performance. To address these challenges, this research introduces a comprehensive SA framework that focuses on robust feature extraction and optimized feature selection for textual reviews. Feature extraction is the process of transforming raw data into meaningful representations that capture the relevant semantics and syntax within the data. In contrast, feature selection identifies useful features from the original set of features and removes redundant and noisy features to improve the efficiency and accuracy of the model.

By incorporating a deep contextual embedding mechanism and an improved sequential learning structure, the model captures semantic and temporal information from reviews more effectively. To further enhance performance, a nature-inspired optimization strategy is applied after feature extraction to retain only the most informative and non-redundant features. This significantly improves the generalizability and interpretability of the proposed system. This framework is evaluated on benchmark datasets to demonstrate its effectiveness and superiority over existing methods. Figure 3.2 illustrates an overview of a workflow for sentiment analysis of text reviews.

The chapter covers Section 3.1 and discusses text pre-processing techniques to clean and standardize the raw input data. Section 3.2 presents the feature extraction methodology, specifying how semantic and contextual information is extracted using deep learning techniques. The feature selection method is showcased in Section 3.3, describing the algorithm employed to select those features that are most informative or non-redundant. Section 3.4 presents the classification procedure for the selected characteristics. Section 3.5 delves into the details of the proposed framework through an example of its implementation. Section 3.6 details the experimental setup, including datasets, procedures, and evaluation metrics, emphasizing how the integrated approach improves accuracy, robustness, and interpretability. Section 3.7 focuses on result analysis, providing a critical comparison of the system's performance against existing methods. Finally, Section 3.8 documents the experimental findings, presenting the actual results produced by the system and validating its practical effectiveness.

3.1 Data Pre-processing

The pre-processing pipeline applied to the review dataset ensures that the textual data are standardized, noise-free and suitable for feature extraction and classification. Initially, all text is converted to lowercase to maintain consistency and avoid case-based mismatches. Punctuation marks and filler words, such as 'umm' or 'like', which do not contribute meaningful sentiment, are removed. The numbers are stripped unless contextually rel-

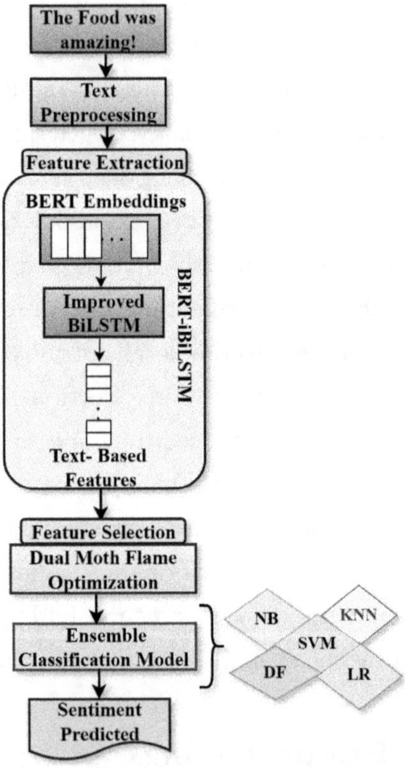

Figure 3.2: Proposed Text Sentiment Analysis System

evant, followed by the removal of common English stop words such as 'the' and 'is' that offer little discriminative value. The lemmatization is then applied to reduce words to their base or dictionary forms (e.g. "running" becomes "run"), aiding in reducing redundancy. Additionally, special non-English or unwanted characters are filtered out and retains only alphabetic characters and spaces. In addition, the function expand_shorthand (text) is designed to identify and replace common social media abbreviations in a given text with their corresponding full forms. It uses a dictionary of shorthand terms such as 'LOL' for 'Laugh Out Loud', 'OMG' for 'Oh My God'. Finally, the cleaned and standardized data is saved in a new CSV file, ensuring that the dataset is optimally prepared for the subsequent feature extraction phase, where meaningful patterns and representations are derived for sentiment classification. This preprocessing ensures clean and consistent textual data. It improves feature quality and supports more reliable sentiment classification.

3.2 Feature Extraction

The proposed system BERT-iBILSTM is the combination of BERT and improved BiLSTM model, which captures both contextual embedding and sequential features. The contextualized embedding is obtained for each token as a unique token ID, represented as T= t1, t2,... tn. This represents the sequence of token IDs for the input text, with n representing the number of tokens. This process then maps each token ID t_i to an augmented, high-dimensional vector. The mapping is performed using a pre-trained embedding matrix W, which is obtained from a BERT model. BERT-base produces 768-dimensional embeddings for all tokens in the input, thus supplying the model with a very informative contextual representation.

The word embedding for token t_i is obtained from the Eq. 3.1.

$$e_i = W_{\text{embed}}[t_i] \tag{3.1}$$

where e_i denotes the embedding vector for each token set. The positional encodings for the ith sequence, represented as P_i, are added so as to preserve the sequential order of the text. The final embedding is represented as Eq. 3.2 after adding positional information.

$$\text{BERT}(E_t) = e_i + P_i \tag{3.2}$$

The embeddings obtained are passed to BiLSTM, which is shown in Eq. 3.3.

$$h_t = BiLSTM(BERT(E_t), h_{t-1}) \tag{3.3}$$

Here, h_t, BERT (E_t) and h_{t-1} refer to the hidden state, BERT embedding and previous hidden state at time step t. These hidden states capture sequential dependencies and contextual information from BERT embeddings. A BiLSTM network combines a typical LSTM cell in both forward and backward directions. This leads to the formation of two sets of LSTM gates: one for processing the sequence in a forward style, from beginning to conclusion and another for handling the sequence in a backward way, from end to start. The following are the equations for the gates. The input gate controls the extent to which a new value flows into the cell state, as shown in Eq. 3.4.

$$i_t = \sigma(X_i\,\text{BERT}(E_t) + Y_i\,h_{t-1} + a_i) \tag{3.4}$$

where, i_t, X_i, Y_i, a_i and h_{t-1} are the activation of the input gate at time step t, the weight matrices for the input and hidden states, respectively, the bias term and the hidden state of the previous time step. The forget gate regulates the degree of forgetting the previous cell state. Eq. 3.5 illustrates the standard forget gate.

$$f_t = \sigma(X_f\,\text{BERT}(E_t) + Y_f\,h_{t-1} + a_f) \tag{3.5}$$

where, f_t, X_f, Y_f, a_f is the activation of the forget gate at time step t, the weight matrices for the input and hidden states, respectively, the bias term and the hidden state of the previous time step for the forget gate. Here, the forget gate is improved in an LSTM by using a ReLU (rectified linear unit) activation function combined with a learnable parameter alpha α, which can bring several potential benefits and address specific challenges in recurrent neural network architectures. The learnable parameter α further enhances this by scaling the contribution of the previous hidden state, promoting better gradient flow. The implementation considerations for the α parameter are that it should be initialized to 1.0 and the range remain non-negative to prevent destabilizing the forget gate operation. Typical ranges might be from 1 to 10, which can be varied based on the specific implementation and constraints applied. The improved forget gate is as shown in Eq. 3.6.

$$f_t(\text{improved}) = \text{ReLU}(X_f \, \text{BERT}(E_t) + \alpha \cdot Y_f \, h_{t-1} + a_f) \tag{3.6}$$

where, $f_t(improved)$ is the enhanced forget gate at time step t. ReLU introduces non-linearity into the model and α scales the influence of the previous hidden state. The cell state candidate represents the potential new cell state, which is computed from the input and the previous hidden state is defined in Eq. 3.7.

$$\tilde{c}_t = \tanh(X_c \, \text{BERT}(E_t) + Y_c \, h_{t-1} + a_c) \tag{3.7}$$

Where $\tilde{c}_t$, X_c, Y_c, a_c is the cell state candidate at time step t,weight matrices for the input and hidden states, respectively, the bias term and the hidden state from the previous time step for the cell state. Next, the output gate controls the extent to which the cell state contributes to the hidden state, as shown in Eq. 3.8.

$$o_t = \sigma(X_o \, \text{BERT}(E_t) + Y_o \, h_{t-1} + b_o) \tag{3.8}$$

Here, o_t, X_o, Y_o, a_o are the output gate activation at time step t, the weight matrices for the input and hidden states, respectively, the bias term and the hidden state of the previous time step for the output gate. The update of the cell state is as shown in Eq. 3.9.

$$c_t = f_t(\text{improved}) \odot c_{t-1} + i_t \odot \tilde{c}_t \tag{3.9}$$

Here, f_t is the forget gate, i_t is the input gate, c_{t-1} is the previous cell state, $\tilde{c}_t$ is the candidate cell state and $\odot$ is the element-wise multiplication. The update of the hidden state depends on the output gate and the updated cell state, as shown in Eq. 3.10.

$$h_t = o_t \odot \tanh(c_t) \tag{3.10}$$

where h_t, c_t and o_t are the hidden state, the updated cell state and the output gate activation at time step t. Finally, the hidden states from the forward (ht→) and backward (ht←) directions are concatenated as shown in Eq. 3.11.

$$h_t = [\overrightarrow{h_t}; \overleftarrow{h_t}] \tag{3.11}$$

BERT-iBiLSTM allows for more effective feature extraction, where BERT captures the nuances of individual words in context and BiLSTM captures the relationships and dependencies across the sequence. This leads to better performance in sentiment analysis.

3.2.1 Significance of Improved BiLSTM with Alpha Parameter(α) and ReLU Activation in Forget Gate of LSTM

Table 3.1 provides a comparative analysis between the standard forget gate in traditional LSTM networks and the improved forget gate that incorporates ReLU activation with a parameter α.

After the extraction of features has been done in a highly efficient way using the improved BiLSTM, the next essential step involves selecting features, where only the most relevant and informative features are enhanced and refined using the DMFO algorithm to yield better classification accuracy with reduced dimensionality.

Table 3.1: Standard Forget Gate vs Improved Forget Gate

Aspect	Standard Forget Gate	Improved Forget Gate (ReLU + α)
Gradient Saturation	Suffers from saturation with sigmoid, leading to vanishing gradients.	ReLU avoids saturation, ensuring stable gradients for positive inputs.
Information Flow	Outputs restricted to $(0, 1)$, limiting information retention.	ReLU allows outputs > 1, enhancing information flow and retention.
Dependency Retention	Struggles to retain long-term dependencies, especially in long sequences.	α amplifies long-term dependencies, retaining critical context effectively (contrastive patterns).
Non-Linearity	Limited non-linearity with sigmoid, restricting the ability to model complex relationships.	ReLU introduces better non-linearity for capturing complex dependencies.
Adaptability	Fixed forget gate behavior, lacks flexibility for different tasks.	α dynamically scales the contribution of previous hidden state, improving adaptability.

The improved BiLSTM forget gate enables more stable learning and better retention of long-term contextual information. This results in more discriminative features for effective sentiment classification.

3.3 Dual Moth Flame Optimization for Efficient Feature Selection

For feature selection, the obtained features are passed to the enhanced algorithm called DMFO, which is developed from the MFO technique. However, conventional MFO employs a single-objective fitness function. The DMFO essentially optimizes two variance measures simultaneously: interclass variance (ITV) and intraclass variance (ICV), thereby discovering an optimal set of features to maximize classification performance and hence the term "dual". ITV evaluates the degree of distinguishing features across classes and the ICV measures the extent of variation within the same class. Considering these two variance measure concepts, DMFO sets the framework to select the most relevant set of features by keeping the intraclass variability low while keeping the interclass differences high. At this stage, the function is minimized, leading to a set with fewer and higher discriminative features compared to the conventional MFO-based approach. The execution of the Algorithm 1 is described below to select the appropriate features to be used for sentiment classification.

The DMFO-based feature selection algorithm is parameterized with the number of moths (N_M), the number of flames (N_F) and the maximum number of iterations (I_{max}). Initially, moth and flame populations are initialized, an initial fitness evaluation is performed and constants like b and t are set. The fitness value of each moth is calculated, the moths are sorted by fitness score and the flames are updated during all iterations up to I_{max}. Then, it refines the position of each moth with respect to the chosen flame using a spiral update function. Later, a new fitness value is calculated and contrasted with a fitness threshold. The best fitness value and its moth are registered so that the algorithm would finish when the best solution is found. Hence, DMFO remains an efficient subset selection technique, which takes advantage of moth-flame dynamics to perform an efficient search of the solution space. Introduced by ITV and ICV, described in Eq. 3.12 and Eq. 3.13, the algorithm ensures that the selected features improve class separability while reducing redundancy.

$$\text{ITV} = \sum_{c=1}^{C} n_c \cdot ||\mu_c - \mu||^2 \tag{3.12}$$

- C is the total number of classes
- n_c is the number of samples in class c
- μ_c is the mean vector of features for class c
- μ is the global mean feature vector

Algorithm 1 DMFO-based Algorithm for Efficient Feature Selection

Input: Number of moths N_M, number of flames N_F, number of features n_f, maximum iterations $I_{\max}$, learning multiplier L_M, ICV, ITV
Output: Best feature subset
Initialize the population of moths M and flames F
Set the initial fitness threshold f_{th}
Initialize parameters such as b and t
  DMFO$N_M, N_F, n_f, I_{\max}$
Initialize moths $M \leftarrow \text{random}(0, 1, (N_M, n_f))$
Initialize best moth $M_{\text{best}} \leftarrow \emptyset$
Initialize best fitness $f_{\text{best}} \leftarrow -\infty$
  for *iteration* $i = 1$ *to* $I_{\max}$ **do**
  end
  Evaluate fitness $f_m(M_i)$ for each moth M_i using:

$$f_m = \frac{ICV}{ITV}$$

Sort moths based on fitness values
Update flames $F \leftarrow M_{\text{sorted}}$
  for *each moth* M_i **do**
  end
  Select flame F_j from the set of flames F
Update position using the spiral mechanism:

$$M_i = D_i e^{bt} \cos(2\pi t) + F_j$$

Calculate new fitness $f_m(M_i)$
  if $f_m(M_i) < f_{th}$ **then**
  end
  Retain the position of M_i **else**
  end
  Replace the position of M_i with new random values
Update fitness threshold $f_{th} \leftarrow \frac{1}{N_M} \sum_{i=1}^{N_M} f_m(M_i) \times L_M$
Find the best moth M_{best} and best fitness f_{best}
return M_{best}

$$\text{ICV} = \sum_{c=1}^{C} \sum_{x_i \in X_c} \|x_i - \mu_c\|^2 \tag{3.13}$$

- x_i is a feature vector from class c
- X_c is the set of samples in class c

Eq. 3.14 is used to determine the fitness of the dual moth based on this evaluation. The objective of the ratio is to minimize the fitness function, resulting in reduced ICV variance, increased ITV variance and a smaller number of selected features.

$$f_m = \frac{ICV}{ITV} \tag{3.14}$$

The fitness threshold value is obtained using Eq. 3.15, after performing multiple iterations of the procedure for N_M moths.

$$f_{th} = \frac{1}{N_M} \sum_{i=1}^{N_M} f_m(M_i) \times L_M \tag{3.15}$$

Where, L_M is the learning rate of the MFO process, N_M is the number of moths and $f(M_i)$ is the fitness value of the ith moth. Using Eqs. 3.12–3.14 the moths with a value of $f_m(M_i) < f_{th}$ are kept and remove those with other values for the next iteration. This process accurately duplicates the features of a moth flame. After each I_{max} iteration, this method iterates to generate new moths, aiding in the identification of a group of features with high variability.

DMFO selects a compact and highly discriminative feature subset by balancing interclass and intraclass variance. This enhances classification accuracy while reducing feature dimensionality.

3.4 Classification

To effectively classify the sentiment of user reviews, a diverse set of classification strategies is exposed that encompasses both individual classifiers and ensemble-based methods. Initially, the performance of several widely used base classifiers, including SVM, NB, KNN, LR and DF, is evaluated. These models served as foundational learners and provided insight into the baseline discriminative power of the extracted features. To improve the robustness and overall accuracy of the classification, these base classifiers are subsequently integrated using various ensemble techniques. The ensemble methods employed included:

- Soft Voting: Aggregates the predicted class probabilities of each base learner and selects the class with the highest average probability.
- Hard Voting: Takes a majority vote among the predicted classes from all classifiers.
- Bagging: Construct multiple models by training each on a different random subset of the training data and combining their outputs to reduce variance.
- AdaBoost: Focuses sequentially on training weak classifiers with updated weights based on misclassifications from previous iterations.
- Gradient Boosting: Build an ensemble of models by minimizing a loss function through gradient descent techniques.
- Stacking: Combines predictions from multiple base classifiers using a meta-classifier (e.g., Logistic Regression) that learns how to best combine their outputs.
- Weighted Soft Voting: It is an ensemble classification technique where the final prediction is made by averaging the predicted probabilities from multiple base classifiers, each weighted according to its performance (e.g. accuracy).

After rigorous experimentation, it is identified that weighted soft voting is the most effective ensemble strategy. This approach assigns dynamic weights to each base classifier based on their individual performance, ensuring that more accurate models have a greater influence on the final decision. The empirical results demonstrated that this method significantly improved the classification accuracy compared to individual models and other ensemble methods.

Let $f_i(x)$ be the predicted probability vector of the ith classifier and w_i be the weight assigned to the ith classifier. Let C be the set of possible classes.

Then, the final ensemble prediction $\hat{y}$ is computed as:

$$\hat{y} = \arg\max_{c \in C} \sum_{i=1}^{n} w_i \cdot P_i(c \mid x) \tag{3.16}$$

where - $P_i(c \mid x)$ is the probability assigned to class c by the ith classifier f_i - w_i is the weight of the ith classifier - C is the set of all possible classes The class c with the maximum weighted sum of probabilities is selected as the final predicted class.

The configurations of the classifiers used are listed in Table 3.2.

Table 3.2: Configurations of Classifiers

Classifier	**Configurations**
SVM	Regularization parameter(C)=1.0 Kernel=rbf , gamma=scale, tol=1e-3 , max_iterations=1000
NB	GaussianNB, var_smoothing=1e-9
KNN	Euclidean distance, weights=distance, leaf size=30, k=5
LR	Regularization parameter=1.0, max_iterations=1000 , penalty=l2,solver=lbfgs
DF	Total Trees (n_estimators): 100, Decision Criterion: gini, max_features=auto, Depth Limit =10 ,Minimum Samples to Split=2

Hence, weighted soft voting was adopted as the final classification model in our system because it not only combines the strengths of multiple classifiers by averaging their predicted probabilities but also assigns higher influence to more accurate models through weighting. This allows the ensemble to produce more reliable and interpretable sentiment scores, especially when fine-grained, probabilistic outputs (e.g., 1.36 rather than just a class label) are required. Unlike hard voting or bagging, which rely on majority class votes without considering confidence, or stacking, which can overfit or produce poorly calibrated probabilities, weighted soft voting maintains balance between interpretability, performance and robustness, making it ideal for SA where the relative confidence of each model matters. The classification model categorizes the sentiment predictions into positive, negative and neutral categories.

3.5 Case Study: Proposed System working on Restaurant Reviews

The working of the proposed system using an example of a restaurant text review is illustrated in Figure 3.3. It is first pre-processed by converting to lowercase, removing stopwords and punctuation and applying lemmatization to produce a cleaned version like "ambiance restaurant stunning food delicious service disappoint slow staff seem untrain." This cleaned text is then converted into dense contextual embeddings using BERT, where each token is represented as a 768-dimensional vector and a sentence-level representation is derived. These embeddings are passed through an improved BiLSTM, which captures contextual relationships and applies a modified forget gate with a learned α parameter to retain key sentiment cues, resulting in a 256-dimensional feature vector. Finally, DMFO selects the 140 most relevant features by maximizing ITV and minimizing ICV , yielding an optimized feature set for accurate sentiment prediction.

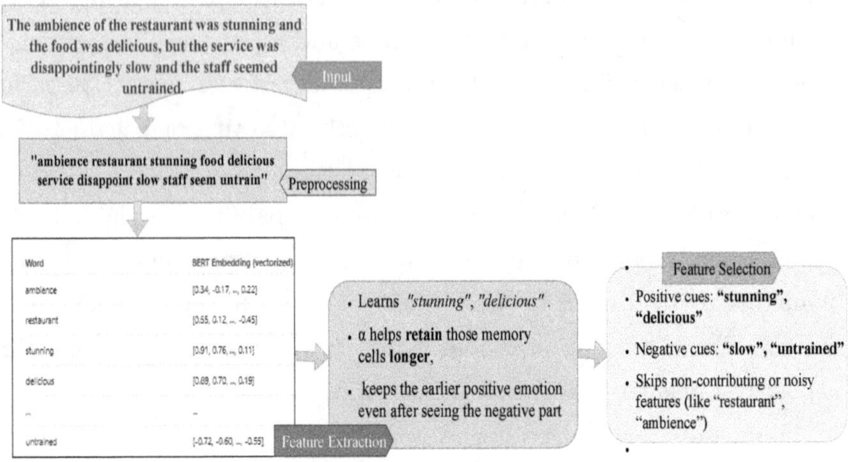

Figure 3.3: Proposed System Workflow Demonstration

This case study demonstrates the end-to-end effectiveness of the proposed framework, from text normalization to optimized feature selection.

3.6 Experimental Setup

This section includes dataset details, parameter settings of techniques used, evaluation metrics and result analysis and comparison.

3.6.1 Dataset Description

- **Dataset 1: Amazon Reviews**
  https://www.kaggle.com/datasets-/danielihenacho/amazon-reviews-data
  This dataset gives an option to train and assess customer product review sentiment analysis systems. It consists of 20,000 user-generated reviews with three sentiment classes: positive (~9,000), neutral (~7,000) and negative (~4,000). Each review data set contains two columns: 'review' with the review text and 'sentiment' labeled 0, 1, or 2 for negative, neutral and positive, respectively.

- **Dataset 2: Imdb Movie Reviews**
  https://www.kaggle.com/datasets/tuannguyen8531/imdb-movie-reviews-for-sentiment-analysis
  This dataset consists of IMDB comments that are utilized for training and testing SA models. Each review in the dataset is marked with one of three sentiment classes: 0 (negative), 1 (neutral) and 2 (positive), which also contains the actual review text. The full dataset contains a large quantity of movie reviews; whereas, in our work, we used a reduced, balanced subset combining 10,000 reviews densely: 4,000 positives, 3,000 neutrals and 3,000 negatives. The goal here was to keep computations more efficient while ensuring an equal representation of all sentiment classes for an unbiased training and evaluation of the models.

- **Dataset 3: Restaurant Reviews**
  https://www.kaggle.com/datasets/choonkhonng/malaysia-restaurant-review-datasets
  The dataset used for SA is restaurant reviews from kaggle which is collected from Google reviews of the top restaurants across various states and cities. The experiments were performed on a total 15k samples : 5k positive, 5k negative and 5k neutral. Like most online reviews, this dataset uses a 5-point rating system. The stars are assigned on a scale from 1 (very low) to 5 (very high). The scores that users give indicate how satisfied they were with their overall dining experience. In this work, the 5 and 4 rating assigned are classified as positive reviews, where 5 stars showed a very satisfied customer and 4 stars showed an overall positive experience ; 3 and 2 were neutral, with 3 stars showing an average experience without major negatives ; and 2 and 1 were negative, with 2 stars showing dissatisfaction, 1 star showing a very poor experience and 1 star showing a very unhappy customer. Table 3.3 provides the sample reviews and their corresponding sentiment labels:

Table 3.3: Sample Reviews with Sentiment Labels

Review	**Label**
Awesome environment! Delicious and affordable meal. Highly recommended.	2 (Positive)
The best roti nan (recommended) & ayam tandoori	2 (Positive)
I love the caramel pudding here, but my must have menu, chicken kebab.	2 (Positive)
Everything is average from food to staff to cleanliness. So, expect nothing special, just an everyday typical local seafood restaurant in a small city of Miri.	1 (Neutral)
Had dinner here on Chinese New Years Eve. Probably one of the worse dining experience. Meagre food, lousy service, plenty of part timers. And very very very over-priced. Definitely the last time.	0 (Negative)

The use of diverse, multi-domain datasets improves the robustness and generalizability of the proposed sentiment analysis model. Balanced class distributions further ensure unbiased training and reliable evaluation.

3.6.2 Feature Extraction and Selection Parameters

The datasets used in the study is split into 80% training and 20% testing. To extract features, the pre-trained BERT model is used for tokenization and embedding, which is then integrated into an improved BiLSTM. Table 3.4 below displays the configurations of the improved BiLSTM used for the feature extraction process. The experiments were carried out by varying the α value in the range of 1 to 10 on different activation functions such as sigmoid, tanh and ReLU, from which an improved accuracy is achieved with the ReLU activation function at $\alpha = 5$. For selecting features, the DMFO algorithm is used with the following configurations, as shown in Table 3.5. The initial feature set contained 256 features before selection. After applying DMFO, 140 features were selected for further processing.

The well-defined feature extraction and selection parameters enable effective representation learning while controlling model complexity. This

Table 3.4: Feature Extraction Parameters

Feature Extraction Parameter	Value/Details
Optimizer	Adam
Learning Rate	0.001
Hidden dimension	128
Loss Criterion	Crossentropy
Forget Gate Modification	Added α as a learned parameter
Activation Functions Tested	sigmoid, tanh, ReLU
α Value Range	1 to 10
Best Activation Function	ReLU (with $\alpha = 5$)

Table 3.5: DMFO Feature Selection Parameters

Feature Selection Parameter	Value/Details
N_M	30
N_F	15
I_max	50
Total Number of Features Extracted	256
Number of Features Selected	140

configuration balances accuracy and computational efficiency in the proposed framework.

3.6.3 Sentiment Categorization Criteria

The suggested model output is classified into three categories: positive, negative and neutral. Sentiment scores are assigned to each category in the range as shown in Table 3.6.

Table 3.6: Sentiment Categories Based on Sentiment Score

Sentiment Score Range	Assigned Sentiment Category
$0 \leq$ score < 1	Negative
$1 \leq$ score < 1.5	Neutral
$1.5 \leq$ score ≤ 2	Positive
score > 2 or score < 0	Invalid Score

The clear sentiment score thresholds provide a consistent and interpretable mapping from model outputs to sentiment classes. This enhances classification reliability and practical applicability.

3.6.4 Evaluation Metrics

Metrics are used to evaluate the performance of a model, which includes fundamental metrics such as precision (P), recall (R), accuracy (Acc) and F1-score (F1). For a more thorough analysis, the Correlation (Corr) and Mean absolute error (MAE) were also computed. The equations for the same are represented by Eq. 3.17– Eq. 3.22.

$$\mathrm{P} = \frac{tp}{tp + fp} \tag{3.17}$$

$$\mathrm{R} = \frac{tp}{tp + fn} \tag{3.18}$$

$$\mathrm{Acc} = \frac{tp + tn}{tp + tn + fp + fn} \tag{3.19}$$

$$\mathrm{F1} = 2 \cdot \frac{\mathrm{P} \cdot \mathrm{R}}{\mathrm{P} + \mathrm{R}} \tag{3.20}$$

$$\mathrm{Corr} = \frac{\sum_{k=1}^{m}(z_k - \bar{z})(\hat{z}_k - \bar{\hat{z}})}{\sqrt{\sum_{k=1}^{m}(z_k - \bar{z})^2} \cdot \sqrt{\sum_{k=1}^{m}(\hat{z}_k - \bar{\hat{z}})^2}} \tag{3.21}$$

$$\mathrm{MAE} = \frac{1}{m}\sum_{k=1}^{m} |z_k - \hat{z}_k| \tag{3.22}$$

Here, tp, tn, fp, z_k, $\hat{z}_k$, m are mathematical representations of true positives, true negatives, false positives, false negatives, actual value, predicted value, total number of data points.

Multiple evaluation metrics are employed to comprehensively assess classification performance and prediction quality. This ensures both accuracy and robustness of the proposed model are thoroughly validated.

3.7 Results and Discussion

The result analysis and comparison section gives a detailed analysis of the performance of the proposed system compared to existing baseline models. This comprises an elaborate evaluation of a number of performance parameters. The objective is to demonstrate the efficiency of the suggested solution and the improvement brought about by the improved BiLSTM, DMFO-based feature selection and weighted soft voting. Comparative results on multiple datasets are provided to demonstrate the superiority of the proposed model.

To begin with, experiments were carried out on dataset 3 to verify the efficiency of different DL techniques for text-based sentiment analysis. Each model has been trained and tested under the same experimental framework using a labeled sentiment dataset, then evaluated using four standard metrics: Acc, P, R and F1. Figure 3.4 elaborates the comparative results among these methods. Among the models, BiLSTM got the best accuracy of 90.18%, followed by better values in the remaining metrics.

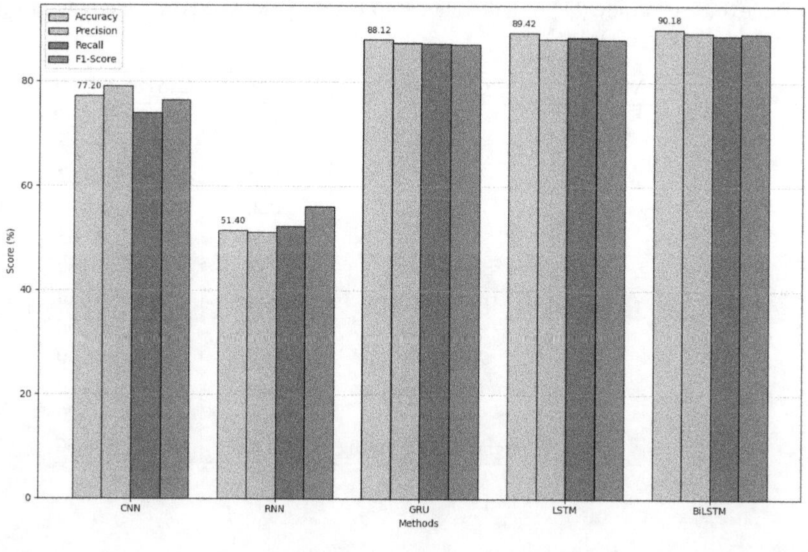

Figure 3.4: Performance Metrics of Deep Learning Methods for Sentiment Analysis

Furthermore, Tables 3.7 to 3.9 show a comparative analysis of various DL algorithms such as CNN, RNN, GRU, LSTM and BiLSTM combined with different embeddings such as Word2Vec, GloVe and BERT for feature extraction across a number of classifiers and ensemble mechanisms. This experimentation illustrates that the BERT embedding consistently surpasses the Word2Vec and GloVe embeddings for all methods, thus demonstrating its flexibility in uniquely grasping finer contextual and semantic differences in text data. BiLSTM with BERT embedding produces the best accuracy of 91.93% on dataset 3 with weighted soft voting, highlighting the power of BiLSTM to capture temporal features in both directions when injected with BERT embeddings. Ensemble classifiers, in particular weighted soft voting, have consistently aided to further ensure good performance in all models and embeddings, proving the superiority of combining several classifiers to benefit from their strengths. In general, this shows that deep models such as BiLSTM with rich embeddings through ensemble schemes provide a very solid ground for text SA without using the DMFO-based feature selection method.

Table 3.7: Accuracy (%) of Different Deep Learning Methods and Classifiers with Various Embeddings w/o DMFO

Method	**Classifier**	**Word2Vec**	**Glove**	**BERT**
CNN	SVM	82.33	83.83	85.57
	NB	78.57	80.83	82.40
	KNN	79.80	81.07	83.67
	LR	80.23	82.80	84.90
	DF	81.97	83.73	85.33
	Soft Voting	83.63	85.12	86.80
	Hard Voting	84.10	85.60	87.13
	Bagging	83.70	85.20	86.90
	AdaBoost	83.40	84.90	86.60
	Gradient Boosting	83.80	85.30	87.00
	Stacking	84.23	85.80	87.30
	Weighted Soft Voting	83.30	84.80	86.50

Table 3.8: Accuracy (%) of Different Deep Learning Methods and Classifiers with Various Embeddings w/o DMFO (Continued)

Method	**Classifier**	**Word2Vec**	**Glove**	**BERT**
RNN	SVM	83.20	84.93	86.77
	NB	79.67	81.10	83.20
	KNN	80.63	82.80	84.07
	LR	81.23	83.53	85.07
	DF	82.90	84.67	86.10
	Soft Voting	85.03	86.07	88.57
	Hard Voting	85.00	86.40	88.50
	Bagging	84.60	86.00	88.00
	AdaBoost	84.42	85.80	87.91
	Gradient Boosting	84.70	86.10	88.20
	Stacking	84.90	86.20	88.10
	Weighted Soft Voting	84.50	85.90	87.80
GRU	SVM	84.00	85.00	87.07
	NB	80.87	82.03	84.97
	KNN	81.53	83.30	85.47
	LR	82.70	84.10	86.67
	DF	83.50	85.67	87.83
	Soft Voting	85.90	87.30	89.40
	Hard Voting	85.60	87.00	88.90
	Bagging	85.40	86.90	88.80
	AdaBoost	85.20	86.60	88.60
	Gradient Boosting	85.50	87.00	89.00
	Stacking	84.13	87.67	89.27
	Weighted Soft Voting	85.30	86.70	88.70
LSTM	SVM	85.03	86.97	88.82
	NB	81.30	83.47	85.31
	KNN	82.10	84.67	86.24
	LR	83.67	85.83	87.96
	DF	84.67	86.27	88.02
	Soft Voting	86.80	88.10	90.20
	Hard Voting	87.13	88.73	90.49
	Bagging	86.70	88.00	90.10
	AdaBoost	86.50	87.80	90.00
	Gradient Boosting	86.90	88.20	90.30
	Stacking	86.60	87.90	90.00
	Weighted Soft Voting	87.10	88.50	90.60

Table 3.9: Accuracy(%) of Different Deep Learning Methods and Classifiers with Various Embeddings w/o DMFO (Continued)

Method	Classifier	Word2Vec	Glove	BERT
BiLSTM	SVM	86.33	87.97	89.97
	NB	82.57	84.73	86.03
	KNN	83.80	85.20	87.07
	LR	84.23	86.37	88.37
	DF	85.97	87.27	89.57
	Soft Voting	88.10	89.30	91.50
	Hard Voting	88.50	89.70	91.80
	Bagging	88.00	89.20	91.40
	AdaBoost	87.70	89.00	91.30
	Gradient Boosting	88.20	89.40	91.60
	Stacking	87.90	89.00	91.20
	Weighted Soft Voting	88.23	89.00	91.93

Later, the BiLSTM is improved by introducing the alpha (α) parameter and adjusting the activation functions such as sigmoid, ReLU and tanh. Figure 3.5 compares the performance of the different classifiers for α values ranging from 1 to 10 without DMFO-based feature selection for the sigmoid activation function.

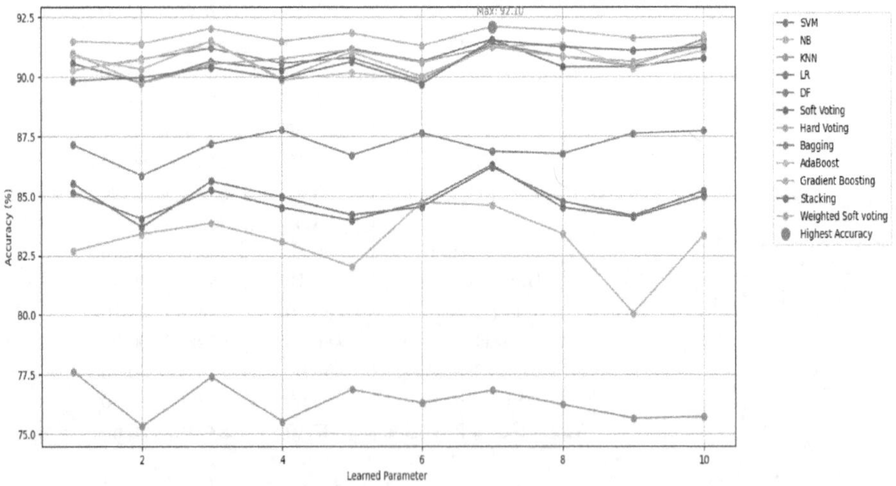

Figure 3.5: Performance of Classifier with Varying Learned Parameter using Sigmoid Activation Function(w/o DMFO)

The performance of the different classifiers for α values ranging from 1 to 10, without DMFO-based feature selection and using the tanh activation function, is compared in Figure 3.6.

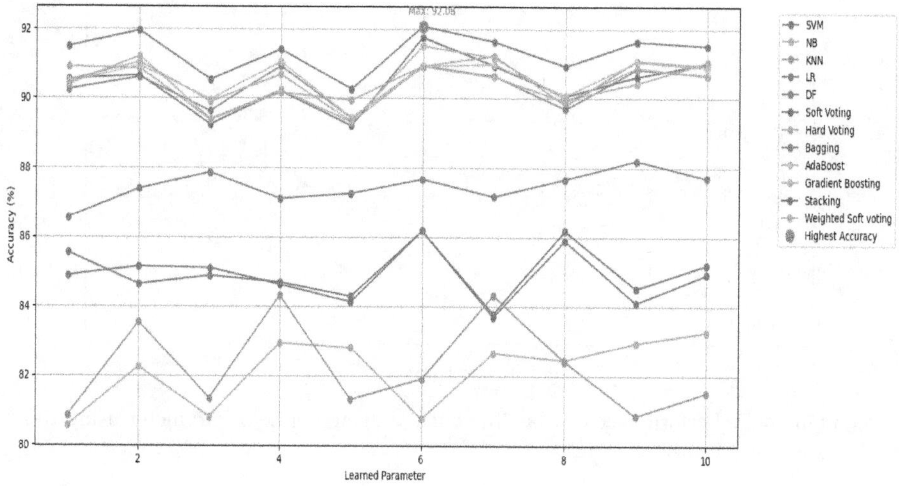

Figure 3.6: Performance of Classifier with Varying Learned Parameter using Tanh Activation Function(w/o DMFO)

The performance of the different classifiers for α values ranging from 1 to 10, without DMFO-based feature selection and using the ReLU activation function, is compared in Figure 3.7. The results clearly pointed out that ReLU activation, alongside $\alpha = 5$, achieves better accuracy compared to all other combinations. This means that adaptive gating and activation functions are essential to control how memory is retained by the units and in modeling time-varying dynamics of the BiLSTMs for enhancing their capability in sentiment classification tasks.

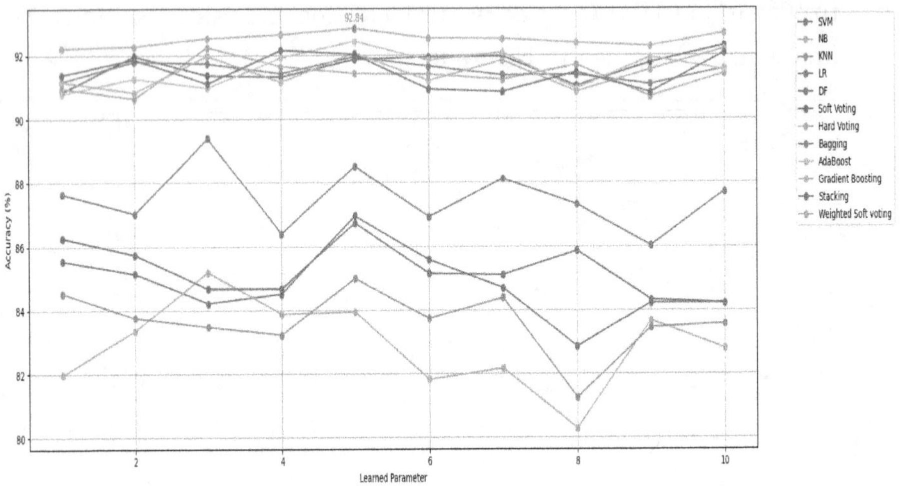

Figure 3.7: Performance of Classifier with Varying Learned Parameter using ReLU Activation Function(w/o DMFO)

To further optimize the performance of the model by selecting the best features, several feature algorithms were considered to test and compare. These included GA, PSO, MFO and the proposed DMFO. In Figure 3.8, it can be seen that DMFO performs better than the rest in terms of Acc, P, R and F1 metrics.

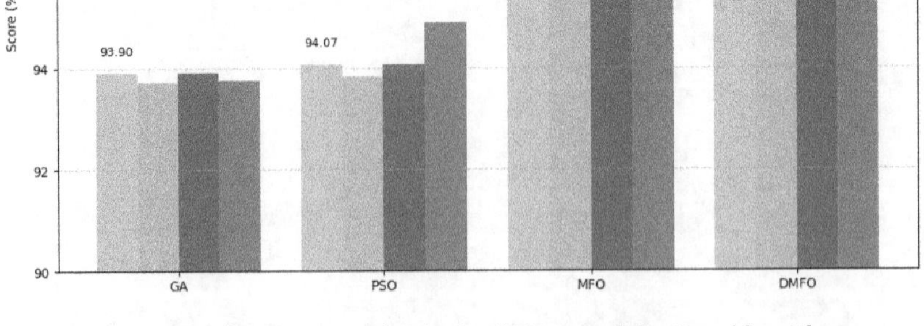

Figure 3.8: Comparative Analysis of Feature Selection Algorithm

The comparison between different DL algorithms with BERT used for feature extraction along with DMFO for feature selection and ensemble classifier weighted soft voting is shown in Table 3.10. It is evaluated on various metrics such as Acc, F1, MAE, Corr and computational speed (Cs). The improved BiLSTM model is observed to be the best overall, as it has the highest Acc (98.77%), P (98.30%), R (98.20%) and F1 (98.25%), as well as the lowest MAE (0.87) and the highest correlation (0.99). This shows that it is better at predicting than the other models. The fastest Cs (2.70) also show how well it works.

Table 3.10: Performance Comparison of Deep Learning Models with BERT-based Feature Extraction

Method for Feature Extraction (BERT+DL)	**Acc**	**P**	**R**	**F1**	**MAE**	**Corr**	**Cs**
CNN	89.37	95.19	93.47	95.31	1.41	0.91	3.93
RNN	90.60	92.06	97.26	93.25	1.53	0.93	4.33
GRU	91.10	97.45	92.53	94.81	2.49	0.94	4.06
LSTM	92.53	93.64	91.89	94.54	1.58	0.95	3.54
BiLSTM	93.00	94.37	95.98	97.07	1.59	0.96	4.24
Improved BiLSTM	98.77	98.30	98.20	98.25	0.87	0.99	2.70

As illustrated in Figure 3.9, the Proposed Model 2 (BERT BiLSTM), which combines the BERT embedding and improved BiLSTM to extract features, DMFO to select features and an ensemble classification model, surpasses all the stated state-of-the-art methods. This system demonstrates its usefulness by achieving the best levels of the Acc, P, R and F1 score, which can be attributed to the use of modern approaches. The notable improvement in performance metrics underscores the resilience and superiority of the proposed system in handling SA for the restaurant review dataset (dataset 3).

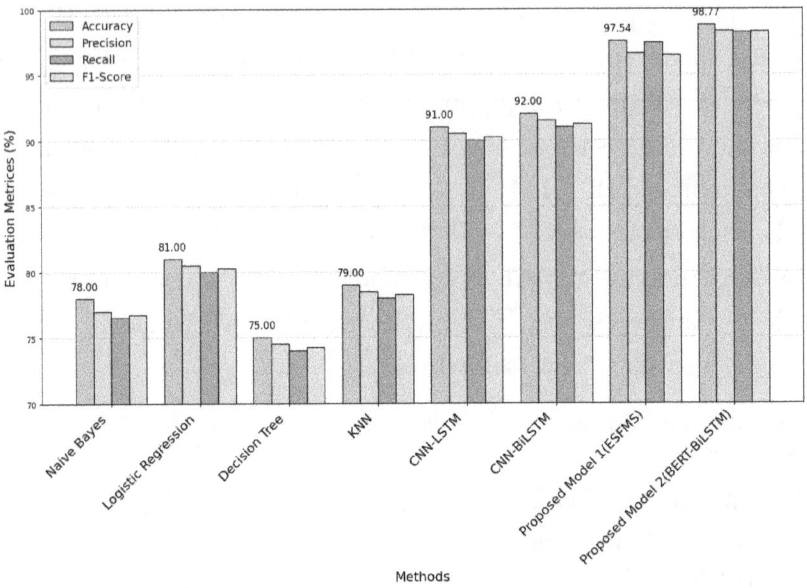

Figure 3.9: Comparative Study with State-of-the-Art Methods

The performance comparison across methods on two benchmark datasets, Amazon (dataset 1) and IMDB (dataset 2), on various evaluation metrics is shown in Table 3.11. Existing models such as LeBERT and NAF-GRU perform relatively worse in both datasets with 82.40% and 86.10% Acc on Amazon and IMDB, respectively. These metrics are much better for LSTM-CNN-GS, achieving 96.40% and 97.80% Acc on Amazon and IMDB, respectively. An additional improvement is found in the proposed model 1 (ESFMS), which includes the optimization of a feature selection technique and achieved 96.62% Acc on Amazon and 98.0 on IMDB. The Proposed Model 2 (BERT-BiLSTM), which combines BERT embeddings with BiLSTM, records the best performances in terms of the highest accuracy of 96.82% on Amazon and 98.22% on IMDB and better P, R and F1 rates on both datasets. This shows that combining the DL method with an optimization algorithm increases the performance of sentiment classification.

Table 3.11: Performance Comparison of Existing Methods and Proposed Models on Amazon and IMDB Datasets

Methods	Dataset1 (Amazon)				Dataset2 (IMDB)			
	Acc	P	R	F1	Acc	P	R	F1
LeBERT [45]	82.40	82.40	82.64	82.52	86.10	86.71	87.00	86.60
NAE-GRU [20]	87.41	88.36	82.17	81.15	91.32	91.37	92.88	91.40
LSTM-CNN-GS [46]	96.40	97.40	99.20	98.17	97.80	98.20	98.90	97.20
Proposed Model 1 (ESFMS)	96.62	97.50	99.32	98.30	98.00	98.30	99.05	97.35
Proposed Model 2 (BERT-BiLSTM)	96.82	97.60	99.44	98.50	98.22	98.50	99.20	97.50

The high accuracy achieved in same-dataset text sentiment classification raises valid concerns regarding potential overfitting. To address this, a cross-dataset evaluation was performed to assess the model's generalization capability under domain shift shown in Table 3.12. When trained on Amazon reviews and evaluated on unseen restaurant data, the model achieves an accuracy of 66.30%, while training on IMDB reviews results in an accuracy of 62.10%. The observed performance reduction reflects differences in linguistic style and sentiment expression across domains rather than model memorization. Importantly, the model maintains consistent precision, recall, and F1-scores, indicating that it learns transferable sentiment representations instead of relying on dataset-specific patterns. These results demonstrate that, although domain variation impacts performance, the proposed model does not suffer from severe overfitting and exhibits robust generalization in realistic cross-domain deployment scenarios

Table 3.12: Cross-Dataset Evaluation Results for Text Sentiment Analysis

Train → Test	Acc (%)	P (%)	R (%)	F1 (%)
Amazon → Restaurant	66.30	65.50	64.00	64.74
IMDB → Restaurant	62.10	61.40	60.00	60.69

3.8 Ablation Study

An ablation study was conducted to systematically analyze the contribution of individual components within the proposed sentiment analysis framework. The objective of this study is to validate the design choices by evaluating performance variations when key components are incrementally introduced.

The baseline configuration employs a standard BiLSTM model for sentiment classification, achieving an accuracy of 90.18%. The integration of BERT-based contextual embeddings and a weighted soft voting (WSV) ensemble classifier improves the accuracy to 91.93%, highlighting the benefit of contextual representation and ensemble learning.

To assess the impact of feature optimization, standard MFO was applied, resulting in a marginal improvement to 92.10%. While MFO contributes to feature refinement, its improvement remains limited due to restricted exploration capability.

The proposed DMFO algorithm was then introduced to enhance the effectiveness of feature selection. This led to a substantial improvement in accuracy to 95.86%, demonstrating the ability of the proposed DMFO to eliminate redundant features and improve discriminative power.

Finally, combining the improved BiLSTM architecture with the proposed DMFO and weighted soft voting classifier achieved the highest accuracy of 98.77%. The progressive performance gains observed across ablation configurations confirm that both optimized feature selection and architectural enhancement play critical roles in achieving superior sentiment classification performance.

Table 3.13: Ablation Study Results

Configuration	**Acc (%)**
BiLSTM	90.18
BERT + BiLSTM + WSV	91.93
BERT + Improved BiLSTM + WSV	92.84
BERT + Improved BiLSTM + WSV (with MFO)	96.10
BERT + Improved BiLSTM + WSV + Proposed DMFO	98.77

3.9 Findings

To further illustrate the functionality and output of the proposed text SA system, this section presents sample screenshots obtained from the implementation. These results highlight the system's ability to process textual input, extract features using BERT and Improved BiLSTM, apply feature selection using DMFO and classify sentiment into positive, negative or neutral categories using the weighted soft voting ensemble method. Figure 3.10 shows the sentiment prediction output for a positive textual review.

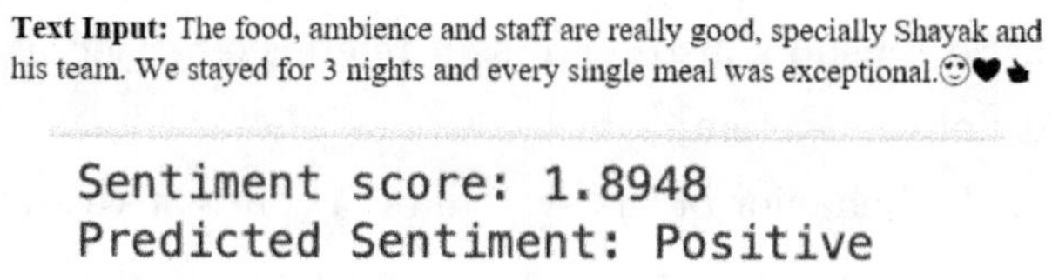

Figure 3.10: Sentiment Prediction Output of Positive Review

As shown in Figure 3.11, the sentiment prediction output corresponds to a negative textual review.

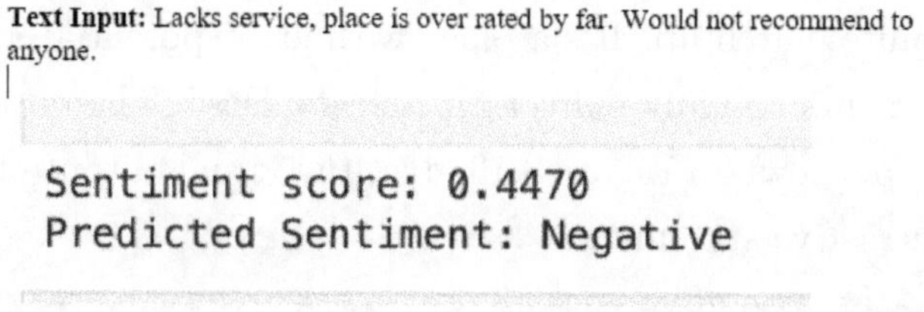

Figure 3.11: Sentiment Prediction Output of Negative Review

As shown in Figure 3.12, the sentiment prediction output corresponds to a neutral textual review.

Text Input: Nice to be on the top... the view of mumbai is awesome. Place is open air and nice music and good crowd. Only drawback is the food, no quality or taste. Would recommend but just avoid eating...

```
Sentiment score: 1.0945
Predicted Sentiment: Neutral
```

Figure 3.12: Sentiment Prediction Output on a Neutral Review

The visual outputs shown above validate the practical effectiveness of the proposed model, aligned with the experimental accuracy results reported. Screenshots also serve as a reference for the usability and interpretability of the system.

Next, the behavior of the system on a contrastive statement pattern is illustrated. Suppose the input statement is: "I visited The Golden Spoon last weekend and while the ambiance was elegant and the staff were welcoming, the food was a bit disappointing. I ordered the grilled salmon, which looked amazing on the plate, but it was overcooked and lacked seasoning. The appetizer came quickly, but we had to wait almost 40 minutes for the main course. The prices were fairly high, but the overall quality didn't quite match up. It's a place with great potential, but it needs some improvements to truly deliver on its promises." The output generated by the system shown in Figure 3.13 gives the visual output of a sample review of a contrastive statement.

```
                    Sentiment Score: 0.6602
Predicted Sentiment: Negative
```

Figure 3.13: Sentiment Prediction Output for a Contrastive Review

In the above input review, the reviewer expresses his thoughts in both positive and negative comments in the same text. For example, it says, "ambiance was elegant," "staff were welcoming," and "appetizer came quickly," followed by complaints such as: "food was disappointing," "overcooked and lacked seasoning," and "waited almost 40 minutes for the main course." The improved BiLSTM with α parameter can handle such contrasts perfectly by retaining the earlier positive cues while still capturing subsequent negative statements so that it can construct a balanced interpretation. It allows the model to weigh both sentiments and make the final sentiment prediction reflect the overall dissatisfaction with the fact that the negative experiences outweighed the positive and turned into a negative sentiment classification.

3.10 Summary

Based on the experimental results performed on dataset 3, several key observations can be drawn. The transition from standard BiLSTM to improved BiLSTM architecture, when combined with BERT embeddings and without applying feature selection, resulted in approximately a 1% increase in classification accuracy using the weighted soft voting classifier. However, after integrating the DMFO feature selection algorithm, the accuracy experienced a further significant improvement of approximately 5%. This highlights the critical role of both architectural enhancements in BiLSTM and the application of an effective feature selection strategy in boosting the overall performance of the text sentiment analysis model. The proposed system achieved impressive accuracy rates across three benchmark datasets: 96.82% on dataset 1, 98.22% on dataset 2 and 98.77% on dataset 3, underscoring the effectiveness of the proposed approach.

In next chapter, a comprehensive framework for SA of images using WaveNet-CNN for feature extraction and DMFO for feature selection will be discussed.

Chapter 4

Contribution 2: A Comprehensive Framework for Sentiment Analysis of Images using WaveNet-CNN for Feature Extraction and DMFO for Feature Selection

Due to the rise of smartphones these days, people have also started posting reviews through images and videos. Considering that 60% of the readers choose content enriched with images and more than 70% of the posts on social networks are visual, there is an emerging need to develop strong techniques for extracting sentiment from images. Expressions, aesthetics and even context play a huge role in shaping public perception and decision making, thereby making excellent image SA techniques crucial.

The general workflow of the proposed system is illustrated in Figure 4.1. Each modality, text, image and video, is processed independently through its respective unimodal model, optimized to extract sentiment-specific features. The resulting sentiment scores are then combined in a late fusion stage, which dynamically adapts to the available modalities and resolves conflicting cues. This produces a prediction of unified sentiment that provides a comprehensive and reliable assessment of general sentiment for unimodal or multimodal inputs. Thus, in this chapter, the image is used as an input for a SA system, where it is independently processed to extract sentiment-relevant features. This module provides visual cues to the overall framework.

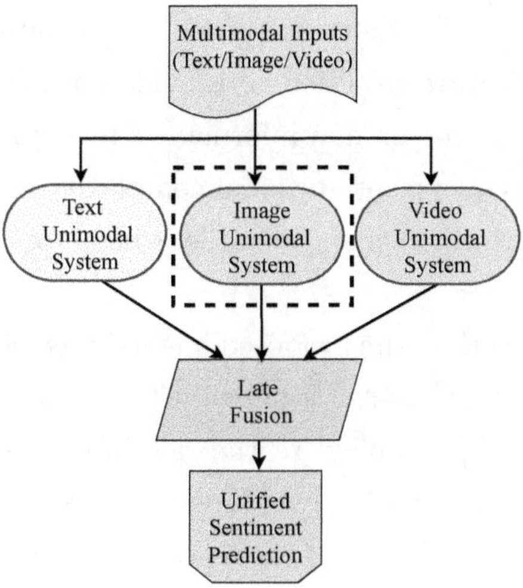

Figure 4.1: General Workflow of Proposed Integrated Model for Sentiment Analysis

The current web is rich in visual content. It allows customers to express their views in ways that words cannot tell [110]. For instance, an increasing number of users began including images in their restaurant reviews. Image sentiment analysis addresses this by evaluating nonverbal cues, such as facial expressions, food presentation and ambiance, providing a more comprehensive understanding of customer feedback [111]. This will assist restaurant managers in tracking customer feedback in real time. By identifying and categorizing the sentiments expressed in the images of the reviews, companies will be in a position where they can easily detect trends or issues, such as negative reviews on certain menu items or poor decor, allowing timely responses aimed at solving these issues. This kind of monitoring improves electronic word-of-mouth management, which has become an intrinsic function in the hospitality business given the competitive nature of this business. Most of the existing systems for SA image focus on a few feature dimensions, usually the spatial features of a CNN. Generally, these work for detecting objects and textures, but most of those spatial features do not capture the finer details, such as color variations or subtle nuances in texture or pattern, which may be prominent in the frequency domain. Furthermore, these models often ignore the importance of integrating feature selection to provide optimized feature sets, thereby producing redundant or non-informative features. This particular set of limitations increases computational complexity and reduces the overall efficiency and performance of the model when crossed onto any varied set of visual datasets.

The framework of the proposed image-based sentiment analysis system is explained in Figure 4.2. It starts with Section 4.1 which describes the pre-processing steps applied to the raw input images to improve quality and prepare them for a further in-depth analysis. Then, Section 4.2 continues with the description of the feature extraction process by integrating features in the spatial and frequency domains. The concatenated feature vector, in Section 4.3, goes through a feature selection algorithm. Section 4.4 presents the classification procedure, in which selected features are given as input to the ensemble-based classifier for the classification of image samples into positive (2), negative (0) or neutral (1) categories. In addition,Section 4.5 describes the experimental setup, outlining the datasets, parameter configurations, and implementation environment used to validate the model. Section 4.6 provides a detailed result analysis, focusing on classification performance and comparative evaluation with existing approaches. Finally, Section 4.7 documents the results obtained from the implementation of the proposed system, highlighting its effectiveness in practical application.

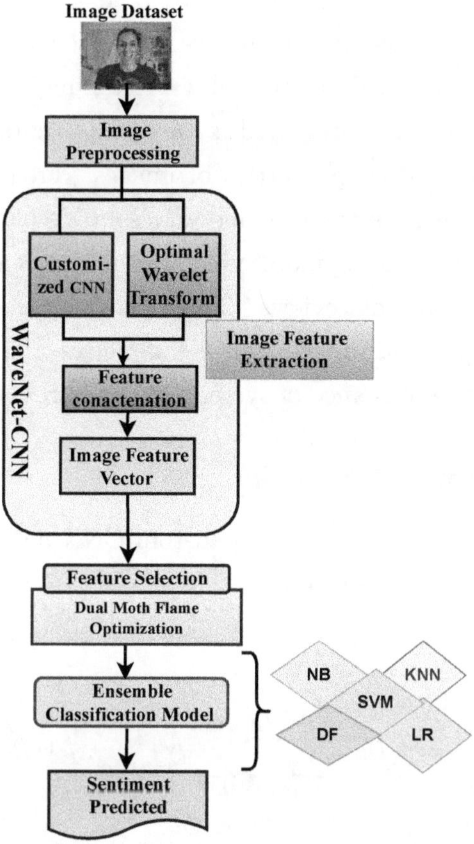

Figure 4.2: Proposed Visual Sentiment Analysis System

4.1 Pre-processing

Pre-processing was applied uniformly to all images, including resizing to 224×224 pixels and normalization of pixel values to the range [0, 1]. This preprocessed image is further processed for feature extraction.

4.2 Feature Extraction

A novel WaveNet-CNN model is proposed that extracts intricate visual features from images, which involves concatenation of features obtained from custom CNN and an optimal wavelet transform (OWT). The feature vector obtained is an integrated feature that accurately captures both the spatial and frequency properties of images. Frequency features capture finer details, such as texture smoothness and color gradients, which are crucial to understanding more subtle visual cues, such as ambiance or food texture, in restaurant reviews. This makes sentiment classification more accurate, more resistant to image differences and more efficient, which improves the performance of systems that use SA.

4.2.1 Custom CNN Model

Initially, the image is passed to custom CNN and the mathematical Eq. 4.1– Eq. 4.6 are given below.

1. Convolution Operation

$$Z_{u,v}^{(f)} = \sum_{p=1}^{P} \sum_{q=1}^{Q} \sum_{d=1}^{D} I_{u+p,v+q}^{(d)} \cdot K_{p,q}^{(d,f)} + \delta^{(f)} \tag{4.1}$$

where:

- $I_{u+p,v+q}^{(d)}$ is the input image value at channel d and location $(u+p, v+q)$,
- $K_{p,q}^{(d,f)}$ is the filter weight at channel d and position (p, q) for filter f,
- $\delta^{(f)}$ is the bias term for filter f,
- $Z_{u,v}^{(f)}$ is the output of the convolution at location (u, v) for filter f.

2. Batch Normalization

$$\hat{z} = \frac{z - \mu_B}{\sqrt{\sigma_B^2 + \varepsilon}}, \qquad \tilde{z} = \alpha \cdot \hat{z} + \beta \tag{4.2}$$

where:

- μ_B and σ_B^2 are the mean and variance of the batch,
- ε is a small constant for numerical stability,
- α and β are learnable scaling and shifting parameters,
- $\tilde{z}$ is the normalized output.

3. ReLU Activation

$$\phi(z) = \max(0, z) \tag{4.3}$$

4. Max Pooling

$$M_{u,v}^{(f)} = \max_{(p,q)\in R} Z_{u+p,v+q}^{(f)} \tag{4.4}$$

where R denotes the pooling region, typically 2×2.

5. Global Average Pooling (GAP)

$$g_f = \frac{1}{H \cdot W} \sum_{u=1}^{H} \sum_{v=1}^{W} M_{u,v}^{(f)} \tag{4.5}$$

where H and W are the height and width of the feature map.

6. Flattening Operation

$$G = [g_1, g_2, \ldots, g_F] \tag{4.6}$$

where G is the final flattened feature vector used for classification.

The CNN architecture shown in Table 4.1 which consists of six convolutional layers, each followed by batch normalization and a ReLU activation function. These are essential to ensure stability and non-linearity. The convolutional blocks gradually increase their filter count from 32 to 512 so that they can capture low-level (e.g., edges, textures) and high-level (e.g., semantic) features. Each of these convolutional blocks is followed by a MaxPooling layer to down-sample the feature maps and thus reduce spatial dimension and computational complexity, while at the same time retaining most of the information. After the last convolutional layer comes the GAP operation, which condenses one feature map into one number, forming a very compact representation of size 512×1×1. This result is then flattened to a 512-dimensional feature vector. The depth architecture of the first-order hierarchy, together with normalization and pooling procedures, ensures efficient learning of features with fewer parameters and yields better generalization.

Table 4.1: Layer-wise Summary of the Proposed CNN Architecture

Layer Type	**Details / Parameters**	**Output Shape**	**Activation**
Input	RGB image input	[3, 224, 224]	–
conv1 + bn1	Conv2d + BatchNorm, in: 3 → 32, kernel: 3×3, padding=1	[32, 224, 224]	ReLU
maxpool	MaxPool2d, kernel: 2×2, stride: 2	[32, 112, 112]	–
conv2 + bn2	Conv2d + BatchNorm, in: 32 → 64, kernel: 3×3, padding=1	[64, 112, 112]	ReLU
maxpool	MaxPool2d, kernel: 2×2, stride: 2	[64, 56, 56]	–
conv3 + bn3	Conv2d + BatchNorm, in: 64 → 128, kernel: 3×3, padding=1	[128, 56, 56]	ReLU
maxpool	MaxPool2d, kernel: 2×2, stride: 2	[128, 28, 28]	–
conv4 + bn4	Conv2d + BatchNorm, in: 128 → 256, kernel: 3×3, padding=1	[256, 28, 28]	ReLU
maxpool	MaxPool2d, kernel: 2×2, stride: 2	[256, 14, 14]	–
conv5 + bn5	Conv2d + BatchNorm, in: 256 → 512, kernel: 3×3, padding=1	[512, 14, 14]	ReLU
maxpool	MaxPool2d, kernel: 2×2, stride: 2	[512, 7, 7]	–
conv6 + bn6	Conv2d + BatchNorm, in: 512 → 512, kernel: 3×3, padding=1	[512, 7, 7]	ReLU
maxpool	MaxPool2d, kernel: 2×2, stride: 2	[512, 3, 3]	–
global_avg_pool	AdaptiveAvgPool2d, Output size = 1×1	[512, 1, 1]	–
flatten	Remove spatial dimensions	[512]	–

Custom CNN draws inspiration from both architectures, preserving VGG's simplicity and incorporating ResNet's optimization efficiency, while minimizing overfitting by using fewer convolutional layers, batch normalization and GAP instead of bulky fully connected layers. Table 4.2 illustrates the comparison of the lightweight custom CNN architecture with well-established deep learning models such as VGG-16 and ResNet-18. While VGG-16 is known for its high feature expressiveness through deep convolutional stacks and ResNet-18 for addressing vanishing gradients via residual connections, both models suffer from over parameterization or high computational complexity, especially in domains with limited data such as restaurant image sentiment analysis.

Table 4.2: Comparative Analysis of CNN Architectures

Model	**Conv Layers**	**Pooling Strategy**	**Pros**	**Why Ours is Better**
VGG-16	13	Max Pooling	High performance, deep features	Too heavy for small/custom datasets
ResNet-18	17 (with skips)	Avg Pool + Global Pooling	Handles vanishing gradients, deep representation	Requires more training data, skip connections add complexity
Custom CNN	6	Max Pool + GAP	Lightweight, expressive, less prone to overfitting	Ideal for multimodal fusion with limited data

The lightweight custom CNN efficiently captures hierarchical spatial features while reducing overfitting and computational complexity. Its design makes it well suited for sentiment analysis on limited and noisy restaurant image datasets.

4.2.2 Optimal Wavelet Transform Model

Similarly, now the image is passed to a biorthogonal wavelet, one of the wavelet types of the discrete wavelet transform (DWT), which is a powerful signal and image processing technique that decomposes data into different frequency components across multiple resolutions. It uses filter banks comprising low-pass and high-pass filters to separate an image into subbands such as approximation (LL) and detail components (LH, HL, HH).There are various types of wavelet that can be used within DWT, including Haar, Daubechies, Symlets, Coiflets and Biorthogonal wavelets. Among them, biorthogonal wavelets preserve the structural properties of organizers in objects such as edges, contours and textures. The ability to retain linearity allows the extraction of discriminative multi-resolution features that represent smooth regions as well as crisp details of high-frequency components. These rich feature representations offer a more capable input for the subsequent classification steps in image-based sentiment analysis, thus improving the performance of image-based sentiment analysis systems. This type of wavelet has two sets of wavelet functions called analysis and synthesis. The analysis function is used to extract the features and the synthesis is used to rebuild the original features. As we need to only extract features, we use only the analysis function. Filter banks are the fundamental components of wavelet transforms, consisting of a low-pass filter (LPF) and a high-pass filter (HPF). Each of these filters is defined by a specific set of numerical coefficients that determine how the input signal or image is decomposed into approximation and detail components. Popular biorthogonal wavelets include bior1.3, bior2.2, bior3.3, bior4.4 and bior6.8, each differing in filter length, vanishing moments and smoothness. In order to reduce computational complexity while maintaining high-quality feature extraction, the HPF and LPF filter coefficients are altered in the analysis stage. This improved wavelet is an optimal wavelet transform and the coefficients altered for filter banks for the vanishing moments v = 2, 4 and 6 as the optimal wavelet filter bank (OWFB) are mentioned below.

- At v=2,
  $Analysis_{LPF}$ = [-66, 115, 425, 247]/512;
  $Analysis_{HPF}$ = [-247, 425, -115, -66]/512;

- At v=4,
  $Analysis_{LPF}$ = [-10/1024, 17/512, 63/2048, -383/2048, -57/2048, 1292/204
  1460/2048, 470/2048];

$Analysis_{HPF}$ = [-470/2048, 1460/2048, -1292/2048, -57/2048, 383/2048, 63/2048, -17/512, -10/1024];

- At v=6,

  $Analysis_{LPF}$ = [-2, 10, 1, -66, 58, 208, -272, -472, 660, 1572, 1036, 232]/2048;

  $Analysis_{HPF}$ = [-232, 1036, -1572, 660, 472, -272, -208, 58, 66, 1, -10, -2]/2048;

These are the values altered and used for feature extraction [101].

Thus, the optimal wavelet transform extracts discriminative multi-resolution frequency features that preserve texture and structural details.

After obtaining features from the custom CNN, the features are concatenated with the optimal wavelet transform to form the vector of image features using the following Eq. 4.7.

$$F_{image} = \text{concat}(F_{cnn}, F_{owt}) \tag{4.7}$$

The concatenated feature vector is then passed as input to the feature selection algorithm to remove redundant or irrelevant features and retain maximum discriminative features which helps in improving the performance of classification and has reduced computational complexity.

4.3 Feature Selection

To select the most optimal subset of features for classification tasks, the fused features are sent to the optimization algorithm named the DMFO algorithm, an advanced variation of the MFO. The feature selection process is discussed in Chapter 3 Section 3.3.

4.4 Classification

The chosen features are categorized using an ensemble classification procedure called a weighted soft voting method. The working is the same as discussed in Chapter 3 Section 3.4.

4.5 Experimental Setup

This section includes datasets details, experimental setup of techniques used, evaluation metrics and result analysis and comparison.

4.5.1 Dataset Description

- **Dataset 1: FER2013**
  https://www.kaggle.com/datasets/msambare/fer2013
  This dataset serves as one of the most acknowledged benchmarks in facial expression recognition, containing about 35,887 grayscale images. These images are gathered from different real-world settings, hence making the dataset quite difficult due to aspects such as low resolution, varying facial expressions and unconstrained backgrounds; these are all scenarios that would map to social media or video analysis. Different emotions are categorized into seven classes: angry, disgust, fear, happy, neutral, sad and surprised. For sentiment classification, in this work, the classes are further combined into positive (happy), neutral (neutral, surprised) and negative (angry, disgust, fear, sad). This grouping indicates that there are 35,887 images in FER2013, comprising 13,287 positive, 6,198 neutral and nearly 6,402 negative samples.

- **Dataset 2: JAFFE**
  https://www.kaggle.com/datasets/tarunparuchur/jaffe-image-dataset
  This dataset is provided by Kyushu University and contains 213 grayscale facial images taken from 10 Japanese female subjects. Each subject presents several facial expressions in a controlled environment. The dataset, though relatively smaller, offers high-quality and clearly labeled expression samples for the same seven categories as the FER2013.

JAFFE contains 240 positive, 240 neutral and 1,224 negative samples of a total of 1,704 images.

- **Dataset 3: Restaurant Review Images**

  The original image dataset consisted of 935 positive, 1,007 neutral and 920 negative samples i.e. total review images collected from various social media and internet platforms and also curated from existing research datasets used in prior scholarly work [63].

  In order to improve model generalization, an augmentation pipeline was applied and the dataset was expanded to 8,790 positive, 9,263 neutral and 8,648 negative images. The augmentation techniques included horizontal flipping with 50% probability, random affine transformations (rotation between -40° to +40° and shear between -10 to +10), gamma contrast adjustment (0.7 to 1.3), addition of Gaussian noise (scale up to 10% of pixel intensity), image sharpening (10%–100%), coarse dropout (2%–10% of pixels in patches) and Gaussian blur (0.0 to 2.0 sigma). Each augmented image was resized to 224×224 pixels. The sample images of dataset 3 are shown below in Figure 4.3

Figure 4.3: Sample Images of Dataset 3

The use of benchmark facial expression datasets and a large augmented restaurant image dataset ensures both experimental rigor and real-world relevance. This diversity improves model robustness and generalization across controlled and unconstrained visual scenarios.

4.5.2 Feature Extraction and Selection Parameters

The dataset was divided into 80% training and 20% testing. The WaveNet-CNN method was used for feature extraction, which is a combination of optimal wavelet transform and custom CNN. This allows for the extraction of complex visual information. To form an integrated feature, the feature vectors obtained from these two methods are combined. The hyperparameters used for customized CNN are the Adam optimizer, learning rate = 0.00001 and criterion = crossentropy. For the optimal wavelet transform, filter banks were used on different vanishing moments (OWFB2, OWFB4, OWFB6). The total number of features extracted from WaveNet-CNN is 1512.

For selecting features, The DMFO algorithm was configured with the following parameters: 30 moths, 15 flames, a maximum of 100 iterations and a learning multiplier of 0.5. The selected features after applying DMFO are 725.

The combined WaveNet-CNN framework enables comprehensive extraction of spatial and frequency features, while DMFO effectively reduces dimensionality. This balance enhances classification performance with controlled computational cost.

4.5.3 Sentiment Categorization Criteria

The suggested model output is classified into three categories: positive (2), negative (1) and neutral (0). Sentiment scores are assigned to each category in the range as shown in Table 4.3 .

Table 4.3: Sentiment Categories Based on Sentiment Score

Sentiment Score Range	Assigned Sentiment Category
$0 \leq$ score < 1	Negative
$1 \leq$ score < 1.5	Neutral
$1.5 \leq$ score ≤ 2	Positive
score > 2 or score < 0	Invalid Score

The well-defined sentiment score thresholds provide a consistent and interpretable mapping from model outputs to sentiment classes. This improves reliability in visual sentiment prediction.

4.5.4 Feature Maps

The hierarchical feature learning in a CNN is illustrated in Figure 4.4. In the initial layers (channels 1–4), the network captures low-level details such as textures, colors and spatial layout. As we move deeper (layers 2–3), the model begins to recognize mid-level features like object parts (e.g., faces, drinks). In the deepest layers (layers 4-6), activations become sparse, with some channels turning dark due to selective feature encoding. These layers focus on high-level semantic information such as identity, object categories, or emotions. This progression enables CNN to learn and represent complex patterns critical for tasks such as sentiment or emotion recognition.

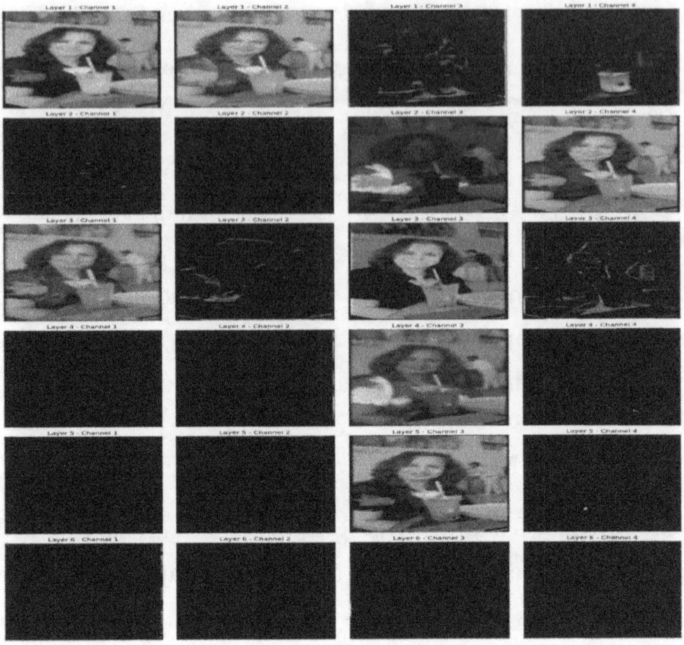

Figure 4.4: Feature Map Custom CNN

The decomposition of an image into subbands: cA (approximation) captures the low-frequency structure, while cH, cV and cD highlight horizontal, vertical and diagonal edges, respectively is illustrated in Figure 4.5. This decomposition effectively captures fine textures and directional details, which are valuable for tasks such as face recognition and food-related images. The model complements CNNs by introducing explicit frequency and directional features that CNNs may not inherently learn, enhancing the overall feature representation.

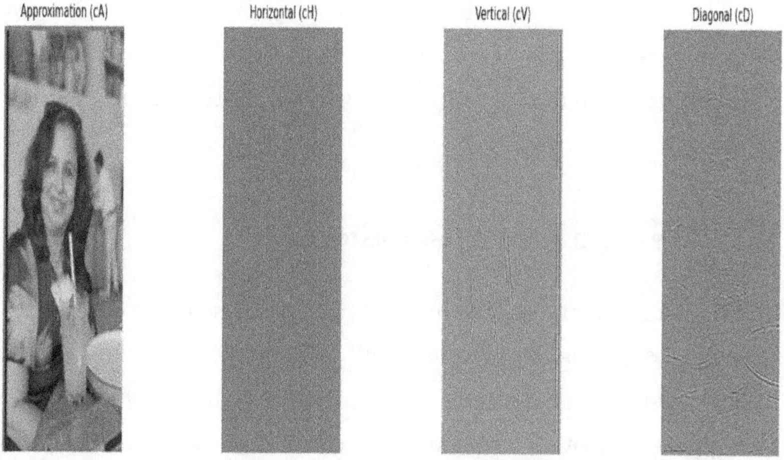

Figure 4.5: Feature Map Optimal Wavelet Transform

The hybrid set of feature maps formed by combining custom CNN output (capturing semantic and spatial patterns) with wavelet coefficients (capturing frequency and edge details) is illustrated in Figure 4.6. The maps are diverse and non-redundant, showing both blocky and smoothly varying patterns. This fusion provides a rich representation that combines deep-learning features with hand-crafted frequency information. In the model, this fused representation improves robustness and expressiveness, improving classification performance by leveraging complementary feature domains.

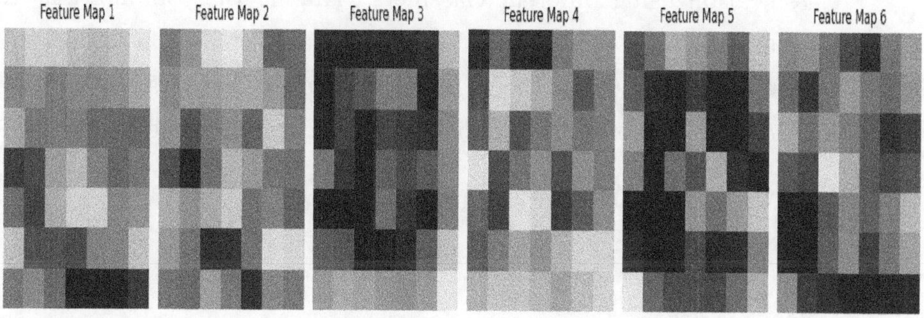

Figure 4.6: Fused Feature Map

The progressive visualization of CNN, wavelet, and fused feature maps demonstrates effective hierarchical and complementary feature learning. This confirms the model's ability to capture both semantic and fine-grained visual sentiment cues.

4.6 Results and Discussion

In this section, the assessment of the proposed system for image-based sentiment analysis is given in detail. The performance is assessed on multiple benchmarking datasets and compared with conventional deep learning techniques and other current state-of-the-art methods. Important evaluation criteria taken into account for the analysis of system performance include P, R, Acc and F1. A critical analysis is made on the effectiveness of components such as feature extraction using custom CNN and optimal wavelet transform, feature selection using DMFO on different classifiers. The superiority and effectiveness of the proposed techniques in sentiment recognition from visual content are shown using comparative tables and representations.

The experiments were carried out on dataset 3, which involves a comparative evaluation between the proposed custom CNN and several established deep learning models, including basic CNN, VGG-19, InceptionV3 and ResNet. These models were used for feature extraction, followed by classification using different classifiers. Among the combinations tested, the custom CNN paired with the SVM classifier demonstrated superior performance, achieving the highest accuracy. The detailed performance metrics of each model and classifier combination are presented in Table 4.4.

Table 4.4: Performance Comparison of Feature Extraction Models(Deep Learning) with Classifiers

Model	Classifier	Acc	P	R	F1
CNN	NB	70.23	70.34	70.00	70.10
	KNN	70.11	70.32	70.30	70.11
	SVM	71.78	71.20	71.00	71.48
	DF	71.50	71.10	71.10	71.70
	LR	71.90	71.70	71.50	71.40
VGG19	NB	71.32	71.01	71.80	71.40
	KNN	71.60	71.80	71.50	71.60
	SVM	72.20	72.40	72.10	72.20
	DF	72.60	72.80	72.50	72.60
	LR	72.80	73.00	72.60	72.70
InceptionV3	NB	71.22	72.10	71.00	71.50
	KNN	72.30	73.00	71.90	72.40
	SVM	73.90	74.50	73.60	73.90
	DF	74.50	74.80	74.00	74.40
	LR	74.80	75.00	74.50	74.80
ResNet	NB	75.50	76.30	75.00	75.60
	KNN	76.30	77.10	76.00	76.50
	SVM	77.00	77.50	76.70	77.00
	DF	77.20	77.50	76.90	77.10
	LR	77.40	77.80	77.00	77.30
Custom CNN	NB	76.80	77.50	76.30	76.90
	KNN	77.00	77.80	76.80	77.20
	SVM	78.84	79.01	78.07	78.07
	DF	77.70	78.40	77.50	77.90
	LR	77.50	78.10	77.30	77.70

Further, experiments were performed making comparisons between different transforms for feature extraction and on different classifiers, and it was found that wavelet transform with the SVM classifier model outperforms them in terms of accuracy. Table 4.5 shows the performance of different transform models and classifiers.

Table 4.5: Performance Comparison of Feature Extraction Models (Transform-based) with Classifiers

Model	Classifier	Acc	P	R	F1
Wavelet Transform (WT)	NB	64.12	62.65	62.89	63.36
	KNN	62.75	61.29	61.76	61.70
	SVM	69.23	67.22	68.12	68.44
	DF	68.17	68.01	68.17	67.93
	LR	64.23	62.83	63.14	63.07
Fourier Transform (FT)	NB	62.22	61.27	60.89	61.52
	KNN	61.12	59.91	60.47	60.56
	SVM	64.56	63.57	63.65	63.11
	DF	65.02	63.76	64.10	64.06
	LR	63.45	62.10	62.24	62.41
Discrete Cosine Transform (DCT)	NB	63.84	62.88	62.35	62.34
	KNN	60.45	59.47	59.45	59.66
	SVM	63.32	62.46	62.80	62.03
	DF	64.94	63.81	63.76	63.44
	LR	62.11	60.98	60.85	60.72
Convolutional Transform (CT)	NB	61.22	60.41	60.31	60.18
	KNN	58.35	56.97	57.74	57.34
	SVM	60.42	59.66	58.95	59.84
	DF	61.77	61.10	61.12	61.11
	LR	60.33	59.38	59.01	59.24

For the WT, initial experiments were performed using base Daubechies wavelets as the mother wavelet at db2, db4 and db6. The results indicate that db4 performs well with the SVM classifier, as shown in Table 4.6.

Table 4.6: Performance Comparison of Classifiers using Daubechies Wavelets

Classifiers	Daubechies Wavelet	Acc (%)	P (%)	R (%)	F1 (%)
SVM	db2	67.85	66.41	66.90	66.65
	db4	69.23	67.22	68.12	68.44
	db6	66.43	65.17	65.68	65.42
NB	db2	61.40	60.80	61.12	60.96
	db4	62.25	61.50	61.89	61.68
	db6	64.12	62.65	62.89	63.36
KNN	db2	61.34	60.70	60.98	60.84
	db4	62.75	61.29	61.76	61.70
	db6	60.42	59.87	60.10	59.98
LR	db2	62.89	61.72	62.01	61.86
	db4	64.23	62.83	63.14	63.07
	db6	61.53	60.38	60.70	60.54
DF	db2	66.74	66.43	66.59	66.51
	db4	68.17	68.01	68.17	67.93
	db6	65.49	65.23	65.38	65.30

Later, the experiment was performed using another type of wavelet called biorthogonal wavelets in a specific biorthogonal wavelet family (e.g. bior2.3, bior4.4, bio6.4). It is observed that the features extracted from bio4.4 with the SVM classifier perform better.

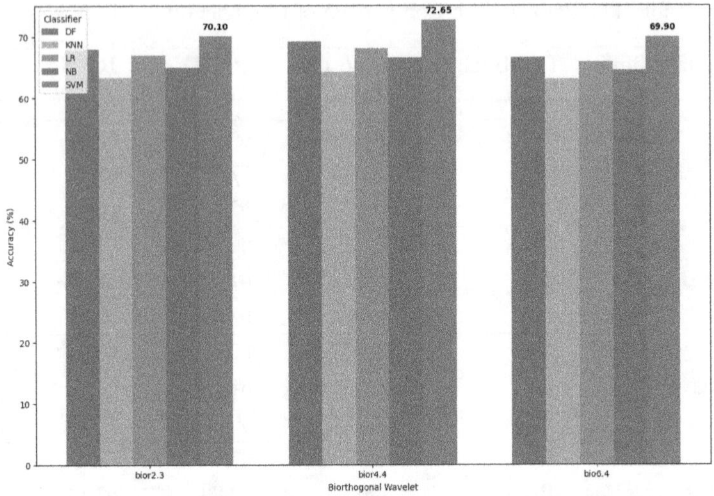

Figure 4.7: Accuracy Comparison of Classifiers using Biorthogonal Wavelets (2.3, 4.4, 6.4)

To improve the accuracy of the model, the custom CNN with the optimal wavelet transform is combined which is obtained by modifying the values of the HPF and LPF coefficients of the biorthogonal wavelet for the vanishing moments v = 2, 4 and 6. Further experiments were performed using this combination on different vanishing moments with different classifiers including ensemble classifiers. Figure 4.8 and Figure 4.9 show the impact of vanishing moment in optimal filter banks on classifier performance without using DMFO. It is observed that as the number of vanishing moments (v) in the OWFB increases, most models show enhanced performance, with the ensemble technique consistently achieving the highest quality outcomes. Higher vanishing moments provide superior feature extraction, enabling the capture of intricate patterns in the data. This, in turn, increases the accuracy and dependability of the classification models.

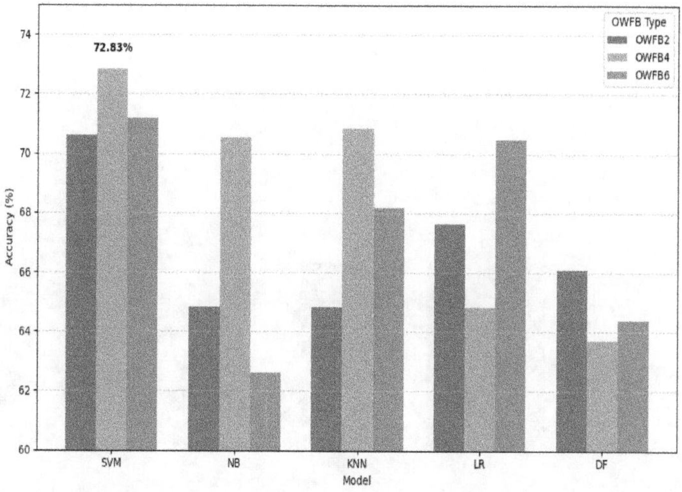

Figure 4.8: Impact of Vanishing Moment in Optimal Filter Banks on Classifier Performance w/o using DMFO.

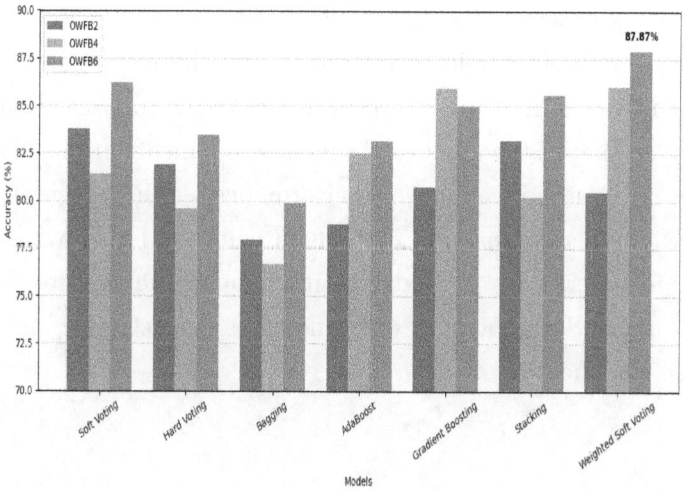

Figure 4.9: Impact of Vanishing Moment in Optimal Filter Banks on Classifier Performance w/o using DMFO (continued).

Then different feature selection algorithms are applied and the DMFO is found to work better. Figure 4.10 shows the comparative analysis of different feature selection algorithms.

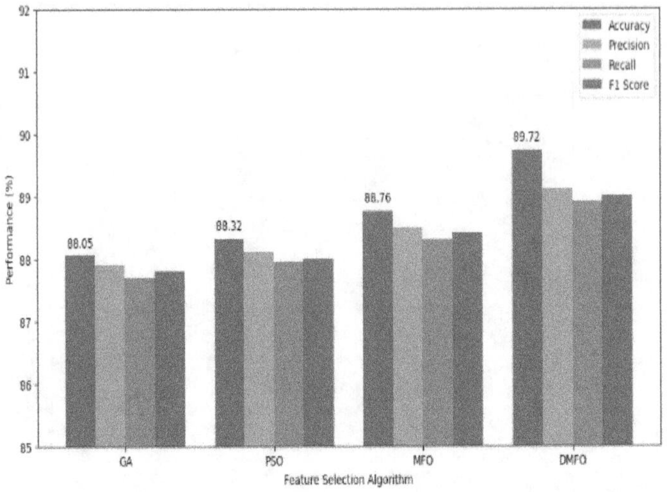

Figure 4.10: Comparative Analysis of Different Feature Selection Algorithms

The performance of various classifiers using a novel WaveNet-CNN method is shown in Table 4.7. This method is a fusion of custom CNN and the optimal wavelet transform where the filer banks are modified at different vanishing moments using DMFO, a feature selection method. It is observed that as the number of vanishing moments in the OWFB increases, most models show enhanced performance, with the ensemble technique consistently achieving the highest outcomes. Higher vanishing moments provide superior feature extraction, enabling the capture of intricate patterns in the data. This, in turn, increases the accuracy and dependability of the classification models.

Table 4.7: Performance Comparison using Optimal Wavelet Filter Banks (OWFB) with DMFO

Models	OWFB	Acc(%)	P(%)	R(%)	F1(%)
SVM	OWFB2	73.61	73.62	72.61	75.94
	OWFB4	75.83	77.91	73.83	71.88
	OWFB6	74.17	74.01	72.17	73.93
NB	OWFB2	67.83	64.91	67.83	64.88
	OWFB4	73.52	77.05	74.52	72.85
	OWFB6	65.60	68.03	65.23	70.72
KNN	OWFB2	67.83	68.49	67.83	67.60
	OWFB4	73.83	77.91	73.83	71.88
	OWFB6	71.17	71.01	70.17	70.93
LR	OWFB2	70.61	70.62	70.61	72.94
	OWFB4	67.83	68.49	67.83	67.60
	OWFB6	73.48	73.52	73.48	73.40
DF	OWFB2	69.09	69.03	69.09	65.94
	OWFB4	66.70	64.44	66.70	72.53
	OWFB6	67.39	67.47	67.39	67.39
Soft Voting	OWFB2	85.76	86.38	85.76	86.14
	OWFB4	87.03	85.03	86.03	86.02
	OWFB6	88.94	87.53	88.94	88.04
Hard Voting	OWFB2	84.87	87.91	84.87	83.56
	OWFB4	82.56	85.18	82.56	83.01
	OWFB6	86.45	89.72	86.45	86.59
Bagging	OWFB2	80.93	75.42	79.83	75.14
	OWFB4	79.65	78.62	75.65	65.54
	OWFB6	82.87	83.44	71.87	72.43
AdaBoost	OWFB2	81.80	84.74	81.80	82.43
	OWFB4	83.73	86.25	83.73	82.88
	OWFB6	86.12	88.95	86.12	86.02
Gradient Boosting	OWFB2	83.44	82.44	82.13	83.12
	OWFB4	83.19	86.10	83.19	84.02
	OWFB6	88.60	88.33	88.60	89.07
Stacking	OWFB2	85.52	87.06	85.52	83.91
	OWFB4	84.42	87.25	84.42	83.96
	OWFB6	89.21	88.01	89.21	88.61
Weighted Soft Voting	OWFB2	86.76	89.38	87.76	85.14
	OWFB4	88.01	88.37	88.01	88.27
	OWFB6	89.72	88.72	89.12	89.71

The comparative analysis of the proposed model with the existing systems for dataset 3 is illustrated in Table 4.8. Models built on the basis of item-orientated CNN and InceptionV3 demonstrate reduced accuracy and F1 scores, which state that these types of model have poor performance in extracting complex cues of sentiment using visual data. DenseNet-121 performs rather well with an accuracy of 89.00% and an F1 score of 87.00% that indicates the potential of DenseNet to represent features. However, the proposed system 2 (WaveNet-CNN) beats all baseline models with an accuracy of 89.72%, a precision of 88.72%, a recall of 88.12% and an F1 score of 89.71%. This enhancement confirms the power of the optimized WaveNet-CNN in extracting and utilizing discriminative features for sentiment classification. Proposed System 1 (MTF), although greatly behind, still shows competitive results proving the robustness of the multi-transform fusion approach.

Table 4.8: Performance Comparison Between Existing Models and Proposed System on Dataset 3

Models	**Acc (%)**	**P (%)**	**R (%)**	**F1 (%)**
Item-oriented CNN [22]	67.80	67.00	67.32	65.80
CNN-based Inception-v3 [47]	73.00	67.20	68.00	68.20
DenseNet-121 [66]	89.00	86.00	88.00	87.00
Proposed System 1 (MTF)	74.80	75.00	74.50	74.80
Proposed System 2 (WaveNet-CNN)	89.72	88.72	88.12	89.71

The comparison of different deep learning models with the proposed systems in Dataset 1 (FER2013) is summarized in Table 4.9. Whereas traditional models such as CNN, ResNet and InceptionV3 exhibit average results, proposed system 2 (WaveNet-CNN) dominates with the best accuracy of 75.15% and an F1 score of 74.36%, demonstrating its ability to essentially extract deeper spatial and frequency features for image sentiment classification.

Table 4.9: Comparison of Existing Models with Proposed System on Dataset 1

Models	**Acc(%)**	**P(%)**	**R(%)**	**F1(%)**
CNN [50]	65.20	73.40	69.40	69.40
Resnet101 [51]	71.90	71.70	71.40	71.40
Inception V3 based model [47]	73.00	67.20	68.00	68.20
Proposed System 1(MTF)	73.50	70.10	68.90	72.90
Proposed System 2 (WaveNet-CNN)	75.15	74.72	75.15	74.36

From Table 4.10, the proposed system 2 (WaveNet-CNN) achieves the best performance among all, with an Acc of 87.42% and an F1 of 87.72%, surpassing Gabor filters, ResNet101, InceptionV3 and even the proposed system 1 (MTF) on dataset2 (JAFFE). This proves to be a great leverage in mixing spatial and frequency domain features for better image sentiment classification.

Table 4.10: Comparison of Existing Models with Proposed System on Dataset 2

Models	**Acc(%)**	**P(%)**	**R(%)**	**F1(%)**
Gabor filters [48]	76.31	72.32	71.92	71.94
Resnet101 [51]	76.44	71.42	75.84	75.84
Inception V3 based model [42]	86.00	82.00	84.00	84.44
Proposed System 1(MTF)	87.34	87.21	86.45	86.24
Proposed System 2 (WaveNet-CNN)	87.42	87.02	87.87	87.72

The cross-dataset evaluation results of the proposed WaveNet-CNN model are presented in Table 4.11. The primary objective of this evaluation is to assess the generalization capability of the model when trained on one dataset and tested on a different dataset. In Case 1, the model trained on Dataset 1 and tested on Dataset 3 achieves an accuracy of 66.30% and an F1-score of 64.74%, indicating moderate generalization performance when exposed to images with different visual characteristics. In Case 2, where the model is trained on Dataset 2 and tested on Dataset 3, the performance further decreases, achieving an accuracy of 62.10% and an F1-score of 60.69%. This additional performance degradation suggests a larger domain gap between Dataset 2 and Dataset 3, making cross-domain adaptation more challenging. Overall, the results demonstrate that although the proposed model maintains reasonable performance across datasets, variations in image quality, expression styles, and sentiment cues significantly impact prediction accuracy, highlighting the importance of incorporating diverse data sources during training to enhance cross-dataset robustness.

Table 4.11: Cross-dataset results for the proposed WaveNet-CNN system

Case	**Train → Test**	**Acc (%)**	**P (%)**	**R (%)**	**F1 (%)**
Case 1	Dataset 1 → Dataset 3	66.30	65.50	64.00	64.74
Case 2	Dataset 2 → Dataset 3	62.10	61.40	60.00	60.69

4.7 Ablation Study for Image Sentiment Analysis System

In Table 4.12, an extensive ablation study is presented which measures the degree of contribution of each component in the proposed WaveNet-CNN framework. The performance of the CNN combined with an LR classifier is 71.50% accuracy; thus, it demonstrates the very limited capabilities of the spatial features used alone. Wavelet-based approaches utilizing db4 and biorthogonal (bio4.4) wavelets get 69.23% and 72.65% accuracy, respectively, which suggests that the information from the frequency domain does help in distinguishing but still remains insufficient by itself. The OWFB6 wavelet on top of that already gives the performance a boost to 73.40%. The custom CNN has a remarkable impact on accuracy and raises it to 78.84%; thus, it reveals its capability for extracting richer spatial semantics. Upon the combination of Custom CNN and OWFB6, followed by WSV classification, accuracy is uplifted to 87.87%. The inclusion of MFO-based feature selection results in a further leap to 88.76%, reflecting that the classifier's power is enhanced through the removal of the redundant and irrelevant features. The full pipeline—Custom CNN + OWFB6 + DMFO—reaches the peak accuracy of 89.72%, thereby confirming that the fusion of optimized multi-domain features and metaheuristic feature selection produces the most effective configuration for visual sentiment analysis.

Table 4.12: Ablation study illustrating the impact of individual components on classification accuracy

Model Configuration	**Accuracy (%)**
CNN + Classifier (LR)	71.50
Wavelet Features Only(db4) + Classifier(SVM)	69.23
Custom CNN + Classifier(SVM)	78.84
Biorthogonal WT Features Only(bio4.4) + Classifier(SVM)	72.65
OWFB6 Features only + Classifier(SVM)	73.40
(Custom CNN + OWFB6)+ Classifier(WSV)	87.87
(Custom CNN + OWFB6) + With MFO + Classifier(WSV)	88.76
Proposed WaveNet-CNN (with DMFO)	89.72

4.8 Findings

This section presents sample results obtained from the implementation of the proposed image SA system. The outputs shown are screenshots taken directly from the developed code execution environment, which demonstrate the sentiment classification results for various input images. These results illustrate the system's ability to classify sentiment categories such as positive, negative and neutral based on visual features extracted and processed using the proposed architecture.

These visual outputs shown in Figures 4.11–4.14 validate the practical functioning of the system and support the quantitative performance results.

Figure 4.11 illustrates the classification of a facial image where the system successfully detects negative sentiment.

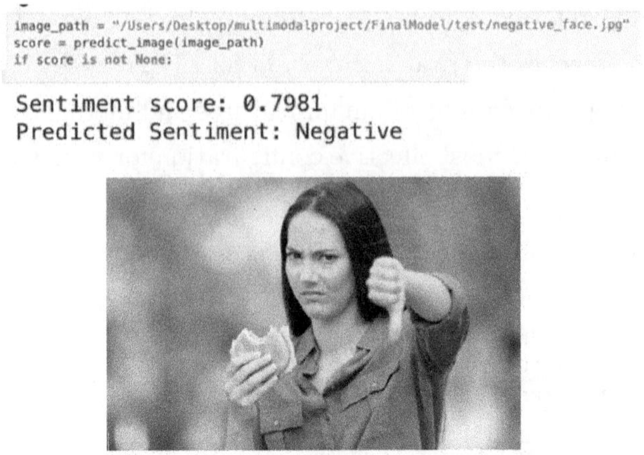

Figure 4.11: Sentiment Classification Result for Negative Image (Facial)

In a similar manner, Figure 4.12 presents the classification of a food image conveying negative sentiment.

Figure 4.12: Sentiment Classification Result for a Negative Image (Food)

As shown in Figure 4.13, the sentiment prediction for the input image is neutral.

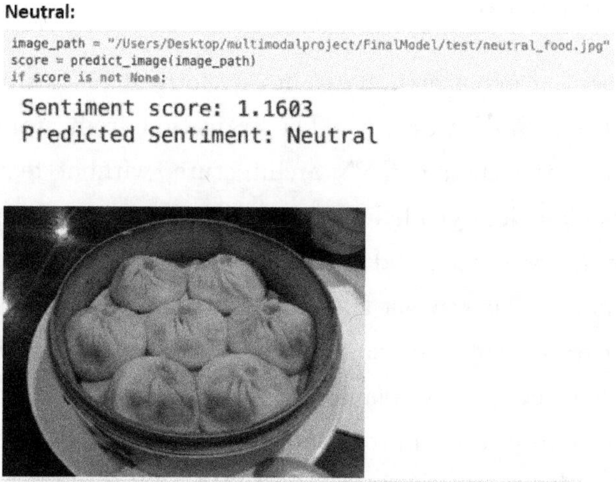

Figure 4.13: Sentiment Classification Result for a Neutral Image

Finally, Figure 4.14 shows a positive classification result, where the system accurately identifies favorable sentiment from the image. This demonstrates the effectiveness of the proposed method in recognizing diverse sentiment categories across different types of visual inputs.

Figure 4.14: Sentiment Classification Result for Positive Image

4.9 Summary

Based on the experimental results performed on dataset 3, several key observations can be drawn. The transition from standard CNN architectures to the custom CNN architecture, without feature selection, on different classifiers yielded an increase in accuracy. In addition, different transforms were compared demonstrating that the WT achieved superior performance. The wavelet transform with modified filter banks coefficients was integrated with the custom CNN to enhance spatial and frequency feature extraction. The WaveNet-CNN model gives an accuracy of 87.87% which is improved by approximately 2% with the integration of the DMFO algorithm for optimal feature selection. This emphasizes the importance of both architectural improvements in feature extraction and the application of effective feature selection to enhance image sentiment analysis performance. The proposed model demonstrated strong accuracy across the benchmark datasets, achieving 75.15% on dataset 1, 87.42% on dataset 2 and 89.72% on dataset 3, validating the robustness and generalizability of the approach.

In next chapter a hierarchical attention-based fusion model for video sentiment analysis will be discussed.

Chapter 5

Contribution 3: A Hierarchical Attention-based Fusion (HABF) Model for Video Sentiment Analysis

In the era of digital communication, ongoing expansion of the internet and smartphones, there is a growing trend of people using videos to convey their ideas. According to statistics, approximately 93% of video reviews are shared on online platforms such as YouTube, TripAdvisor, Yelp and Instagram, showing the increasing significance of video content. Figure 5.1 shows the general workflow of the proposed system that addresses each modality independently by first processing each modality through respective unimodal models for text, image and video, each optimized for extracting sentiment-specific features. The resulting sentiment scores are then combined in a late fusion stage, which dynamically adapts to the available modalities and resolves conflicting cues. This produces a prediction of unified sentiment that provides a comprehensive and reliable assessment of general sentiment for unimodal, bimodal, or multimodal inputs. Thus, in this chapter, video is fed as an input to analysis system of sentiments, where the data is independently processed to extract sentiment-relevant features across various modalities, i.e., visual frames, audio and textual transcripts. This module captures dynamic and contextual cues for rich multimodal information within the entire framework.

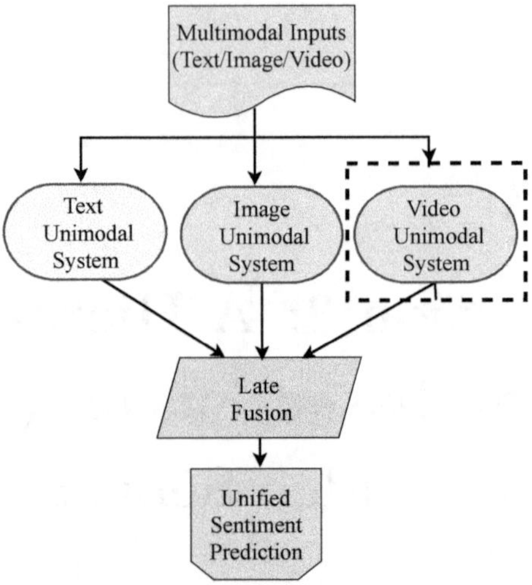

Figure 5.1: General Workflow of Proposed Integrated Model for Sentiment Analysis

Despite the growing prevalence of video reviews, traditional SA focuses on analyzing text or image reviews, providing a limited perspective. Hence, there is a need to analyze videos that contain multiple modalities, such as transcripts (text), audio and visual data. This led to the emergence of multimodal sentiment analysis, which is capable of fusion of these modalities and providing a deeper understanding of sentiment [109]. The multimodal data offer both an opportunity and a difficulty for MSA. Although it enhances existing knowledge, the diverse nature of data presents substantial challenges when it comes to fusion. The challenge becomes even more pronounced in scenarios where the modalities present conflicting signals. A customer may verbally express dissatisfaction with phrases like "the service was slow" while maintaining a calm tone and a neutral or smiling facial expression. Although most current fusion strategies, such as early, late, intermediate and hybrid fusion, suffer from significant drawbacks. Early fusion may overfit due to the concatenation of raw features; late fusion often ignores interdependencies between modalities as they are classified separately; and hybrid strategies aim to bridge both approaches by combining, but generally do not exploit multimodal data's differential nature to a full extent. Thus, these methods often fail to effectively resolve the conflict, leading to a significant deficiency in the accuracy and comprehensiveness of SA in multimodal data. Therefore, it is important to extract features from the different modalities and to use beneficial fusion algorithms. Furthermore, most of the research available with MSA is concerned with general-purpose datasets that do not capture the nuances of specific domains, such as restaurant reviews. People often visit different restaurants and post reviews in the form of text, images, or videos on websites such as TripAdvisor, Zomato, Yelp and Google Reviews as feedback expressing their thoughts about food quality, ambiance and service.

The above mentioned gaps give the motivation for two major improvements: the development of a specialized domain-specific video dataset that correctly represents genuine user feedback, more so in areas like fine dining and restaurants, and the design of strong fusion mechanisms that prioritize and integrate features in modalities dynamically, focusing especially on modeling interdependency that can solve modality conflicts effectively. It starts with the pre-processing steps applied to the input videos, which included the extraction of frames, audio and transcripts for multimodal analysis. Section 5.1 continues with feature extraction of text, visual and audio, respectively, using different techniques. Section 5.2 discusses the integration of modality-specific features using proposed fusion technique HABF. In Section 5.3, the classification part is discussed, where fused features are fed into a variety of classifiers with the task of classifying the video into one of the sentiment classes: positive (2), negative (0) or neutral (1). Section 5.4 describes the experimental setup for assessing the video SA system, while Section 5.5 discusses the results and merits of the proposed method. Section 5.6 illustrates the outputs of the implemented system with visualization and predictions based on real video inputs, thus solidifying the practical potency of the proposed solution.

The workflow of the proposed system is shown in Figure 5.2. Initially, video is ingested into the system; the audio file is extracted from a video using the moviepy library and saved as .wav file. This audio is then transcribed into text using the SpeechRecognition library with Google Speech-to-Text providing a transcript for further analysis. For visual data, the OpenCV library is used to extract frames from video files, saving the frames in a specified output folder. The `'extractframes'` function takes the path of the video file and the output folder as input, reads the video, calculates the frame rate and extracts one frame per second. The text (X_{text}), audio (X_{audio}) and visual (X_{visual}) data obtained are individually passed to the respective unimodal feature extraction module for further processing. The individual features generated ($X'_{text}, X'_{audio} and X'_{visual}$) are fused together using a novel Hierarchical Attention-Based Fusion (HABF), which is an early fusion technique also called feature-level fusion, explained in Section 3.2. These integrated features are passed on to a classification model to predict the final sentiment as positive, negative, or neutral. The detailed explanation of the proposed system is given below:

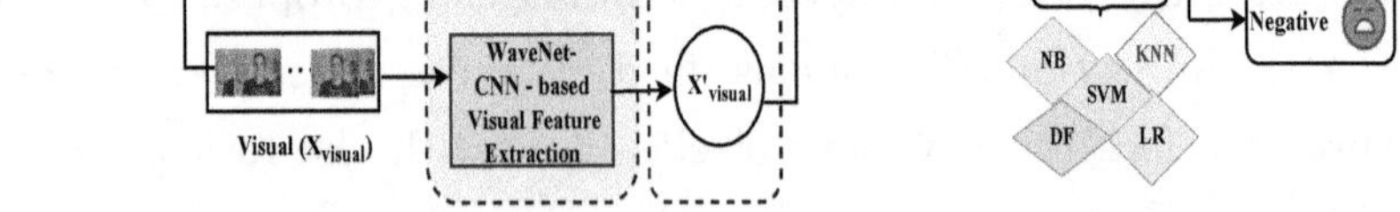

Figure 5.2: Workflow of the Proposed System

5.1 Feature Extraction

In the proposed system, the extraction of features plays a crucial role because it helps to extract the essential characteristics from the text (X_{text}), audio (X_{audio}) and visual (X_{visual}) data obtained from video files. The unimodal feature extraction module then receives this information, extracting a feature from each modality using the detailed methods outlined in Sections 5.2.1 to 5.2.3.

5.1.1 Text Feature Extraction using BERT-iBiLSTM

For text feature extraction, the technique used is similar to that discussed in Chapter 3, Section 3.2.

5.1.2 Visual Feature Extraction using WaveNet-CNN

For image or visual feature extraction, the technique used is similar to that discussed in Chapter 4, Section 4.2.

Finally, the features of all the video frames are aggregated to form a comprehensive representation of the visual modality. Frame aggregation is achieved by computing the average of features in all frames per video. This step ensures that the temporal information across frames is captured effectively while reducing the feature dimensions to a single vector representing the entire video.

Facial expressions and gestures are important visual features that carry emotional nuances to facilitate SA. Positive facial features such as smiles and raised eyebrows represent pleasure or approval; negative ones, such as frowns and tight lips, dissatisfy or worry, while neutral facial features, by their nature, exhibit the least emotion with relaxed facial expression. Then, such features would be analyzed to understand the emotional context communicated by facial expressions and gestures, which would now further enrich the entire SA process. Through observation of these positive, negative and neutral facial features, the interpretation of the emotional context will then be effective, thereby making a great enrichment to the entire process of SA.

5.1.3 Audio Feature Extraction using Librosa

From the video file, an audio modality X_{audio} .wav file is generated and additional audio features are extracted using these files in a specified folder. For training purposes, all .wav files in the folder are recursively processed. The `extract_audio_features` function uses Librosa to load each audio file and compute various features, including MFCCs (13 coefficients),chroma features (12 bins), centroid, spectral bandwidth, RMS (energy) and zero-crossing rate. All these features are calculated using the following Eq. 5.1–Eq. 5.5.

$$\text{MFCC}_i = \text{DCT}(\log(\text{Mel-filterbank}(X_{\text{audio}}))) \tag{5.1}$$

$$\text{Centroid} = \frac{\sum_f f \cdot P(f)}{\sum_f P(f)} \tag{5.2}$$

$$\text{Bandwidth} = \sqrt{\frac{\sum_f (f - \text{Centroid})^2 \cdot P(f)}{\sum_f P(f)}} \tag{5.3}$$

$$\text{RMS} = \sqrt{\frac{1}{T}\sum_{t=1}^{T} x_t^2} \tag{5.4}$$

$$\text{ZCR} = \frac{1}{T}\sum_{t=1}^{T-1} \mathbb{1}[x_t \cdot x_{t+1} < 0] \tag{5.5}$$

This ensures that the audio features X'_{audio} of all files are efficiently extracted and stored.

Further, the extracted features for each modality are X'_{text}, X'_{audio}, X'_{visual}, which are subsequently used for fusion and classification.

5.2 Hierarchical Attention-based Fusion

In MSA, to preserve the conceptual integrity of different modalities, fusion plays an important role. There are three categories of fusion feature-based (early fusion), fusion in the middle stage (intermediate fusion) and fusion in the last step also called as decision-based (late fusion). For our work, we choose early fusion as it enables the system to achieve a deeper and richer understanding of user sentiment by concatenating features from multiple modalities (e.g., text, audio and visual) into a single feature vector which is then passed to a classifier for prediction. However, traditional fusion methods often involve a simple concatenation of features, failing to adapt dynamically to the varying importance of each modality. Wherein the novel HABF dynamically assigns attention weights to each modality based on its contextual relevance, ensuring that the most important modality contributes more to the final decision, reducing redundancy and improving interpretability.

Figure 5.3 shows a comprehensive and systematic explanation of the system. The features extracted as X'_{text}, X'_{audio} and X'_{visual} from text, audio and visual individually are passed on for early fusion using HABF, which combines features from various modalities in a systematic way. This approach initially employs self-attention inside each modality (intra-modality attention) to capture interdependencies within the same modality. Next, it utilizes cross-attention (inter-modality attention) to capture the interdependencies among various modalities. Ultimately, the aggregated characteristics undergo processing through a fully connected layer to generate the ultimate fused representation. Further, these fused features are passed for classification. The detailed explanation of the method is given below.

5.2.1 Self-Attention (Intra-Modality Attention)

For each modality,the extracted features X'_{text}, X'_{audio} and X'_{visual} self-attention are applied to capture dependencies within the modality.

- **Self-Attention for Text Features**

  For text features X'_{text}, initially the hidden dimension is projected which allows the model to apply self-attention mechanisms and capturing contextual relationships within the text modality effectively as show in Eq.5.6.

$$H_{\text{text}} = W_{\text{proj,text}} X'_{\text{text}} \tag{5.6}$$

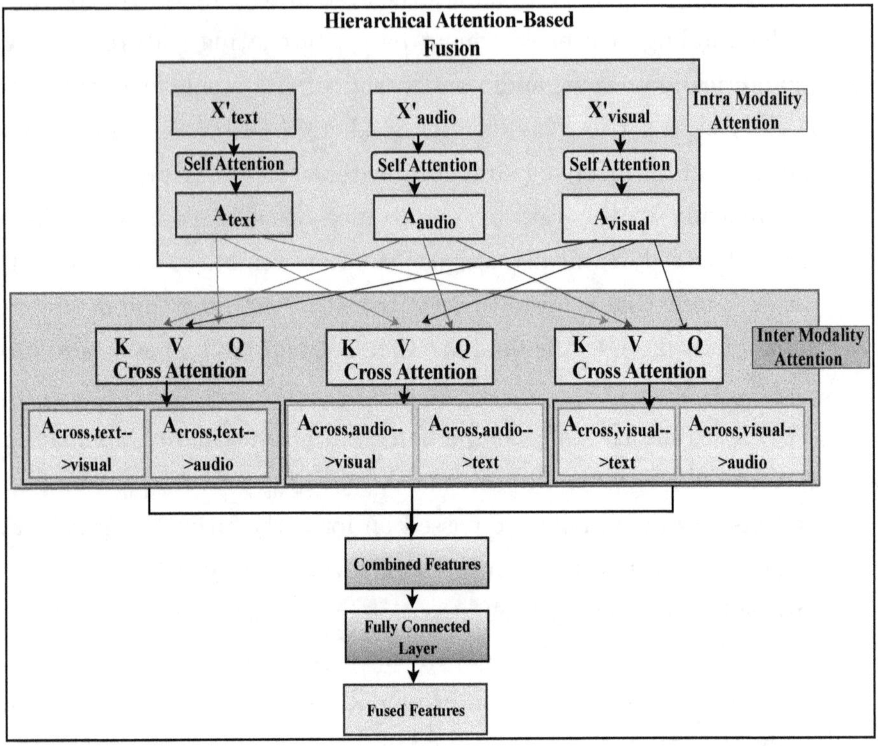

Figure 5.3: Architecture of Hierarchical Attention-Based Fusion(HABF)

Here, X'_{text} is the input feature matrix for the text modality such that each row corresponds to a feature vector representing a word or token. This matrix projects into hidden space using a learnable weight matrix $W_{\text{proj,text}}$, resulting in H_{text}. Dimensions of H_{text} would be entirely $n \times d_{\text{hidden}}$, where n refers to the number of tokens and d_{hidden} is the dimensionality of the hidden space. Further, the projected feature matrix H_{text} is transformed into query (Q_{text}), key (K_{text}), and value (V_{text}) matrices using learnable weight matrices W_Q, W_K, and W_V, respectively. These transformations facilitate the computation of attention scores and the generation of weighted representations within the text modality as shown in Eq. 5.7.

$$Q_{\text{text}} = W_Q H_{\text{text}}, K_{\text{text}} = W_K H_{\text{text}}, V_{\text{text}} = W_V H_{\text{text}} \tag{5.7}$$

To derive the self-attended representation A_{text}, the similarity between tokens is calculated by a dot product $Q_{\text{text}} K_{\text{text}}^T$. It is then scaled down by the factor of $\sqrt{d_{\text{hidden}}}$ so as to avoid very large numbers, which could lead to vanishing gradients during the training process. The softmax function is then applied to score these values to normalize them into high-probability distributions for the most relevant tokens. Finally, this result is multiplied with the normalized scores by V_{text}, as demonstrated in Eq. 5.8.

$$A_{\text{text}} = \text{softmax}\left(\frac{Q_{\text{text}} K_{\text{text}}^T}{\sqrt{d_{\text{hidden}}}}\right) V_{\text{text}} \tag{5.8}$$

- **Self-Attention for Visual and Audio Features**
  The projected feature matrices H_{visual} and H_{audio} as shown in Eq .5.9 and Eq. 5.12 respectively is computed for visual and audio modalities. The projection matrices are converted to query (Q), key (K) and value (V) matrices using learnable weight matrices W for query (audio or visual) as shown in Eq. 5.10 and Eq. 5.13. These configurations enable the computation of attention score and the generation of attention-weighted representations in each modality. The similarity between elements (such as visual regions or audio frames) is determined by the dot product QK^T. To prevent excessively large values that could lead to vanishing gradients during training, this result is scaled by dividing by $\sqrt{d_{\text{hidden}}}$, where d_{hidden} is the dimensionality of the hidden space. Applying the softmax function to the scaled scores normalizes them into a probability distribution, highlighting the most relevant elements. Finally, multiplying these normalized scores by V aggregates the value vectors, weighted by their relevance, to produce the self-attended representations A_{visual} and A_{audio} for the visual and

audio modalities, respectively as shown in Eqs. 5.11 and 5.14 respectively.

$$H_{\text{visual}} = W_{\text{proj,visual}} X'_{\text{visual}} \tag{5.9}$$

$$Q_{\text{visual}} = W_Q H_{\text{visual}}, K_{\text{visual}} = W_K H_{\text{visual}}, V_{\text{visual}} = W_V H_{\text{visual}} \tag{5.10}$$

$$A_{\text{visual}} = \text{softmax}\left(\frac{Q_{\text{visual}} K_{\text{visual}}^T}{\sqrt{d_{\text{hidden}}}}\right) V_{\text{visual}} \tag{5.11}$$

$$H_{\text{audio}} = W_{\text{proj,audio}} X'_{\text{audio}} \tag{5.12}$$

$$Q_{\text{audio}} = W_Q H_{\text{audio}}, K_{\text{audio}} = W_K H_{\text{audio}}, V_{\text{audio}} = W_V H_{\text{audio}} \tag{5.13}$$

$$A_{\text{audio}} = \text{softmax}\left(\frac{Q_{\text{audio}} K_{\text{audio}}^T}{\sqrt{d_{\text{hidden}}}}\right) V_{\text{audio}} \tag{5.14}$$

5.2.2 Cross-Attention (Inter-Modality Attention)

Cross-Attention integrates features across multiple modalities, emphasizing inter-modality dependencies. For inter-modality attention the outputs obtained from intra-modality A_{text}, A_{audio} and A_{visual} are used as inputs for cross-attention to integrate features from all modalities.

- **Cross-Attention for Text Querying Visual and Audio Features**

  The cross-attention uses text features as queries to attend to visual and audio features. This enables the model to focus on relevant parts of the visual and audio based on the content of the text. This is achieved by following steps.

  1. **Text Querying Visual Features**

     Given the self-attended representations for text (A_{text}) and visual (A_{visual}) modalities, the cross-attention where text features act as queries to visual features are computed in Eq. 5.15.

$$Q_{\text{text}} = W_Q A_{\text{text}}, K_{\text{visual}} = W_K A_{\text{visual}}, V_{\text{visual}} = W_V A_{\text{visual}} \tag{5.15}$$

     where, W_Q, W_K and W_V are learnable weight matrices. The cross-attended representation is then computed as in Eq. 5.16.

$$A_{\text{cross,text}\rightarrow\text{visual}} = \text{softmax}\left(\frac{Q_{\text{text}}K_{\text{visual}}^{\top}}{\sqrt{d_{\text{hidden}}}}\right)V_{\text{visual}} \tag{5.16}$$

where, d_{hidden} is the dimensionality of the hidden space.

2. **Text Querying Audio Features**

   Similarly, text features act as queries to audio features is computed using Eq. 5.17. The cross-attended representation is achieved using Eq. 5.18.

$$K_{\text{audio}} = W_K A_{\text{audio}}, V_{\text{audio}} = W_V A_{\text{audio}} \tag{5.17}$$

$$A_{\text{cross,text}\rightarrow\text{audio}} = \text{softmax}\left(\frac{Q_{\text{text}}K_{\text{audio}}^{\top}}{\sqrt{d_{\text{hidden}}}}\right)V_{\text{audio}} \tag{5.18}$$

- **Cross-attention for Audio Querying Text and Visual Features**

1. **Audio Querying Text Features**

   The cross-attention where audio features act as queries to text and visual features are computed in Eq. 5.19 and the cross-attended representation is calculated by Eq. 5.20.

$$Q_{\text{audio}} = W_Q A_{\text{audio}}, K_{\text{text}} = W_K A_{\text{text}}, V_{\text{text}} = W_V A_{\text{text}} \tag{5.19}$$

$$A_{\text{cross,audio}\rightarrow\text{text}} = \text{softmax}\left(\frac{Q_{\text{audio}}K_{\text{text}}^{\top}}{\sqrt{d_{\text{hidden}}}}\right)V_{\text{text}} \tag{5.20}$$

2. **Audio Querying Visual Features**

   Similarly, audio features querying visual features is computed using Eq. 5.21. The cross-attended representation is achieved using Eq. 5.22.

$$K_{\text{visual}} = W_K A_{\text{visual}}, V_{\text{visual}} = W_V A_{\text{visual}} \tag{5.21}$$

$$A_{\text{cross,audio}\rightarrow\text{visual}} = \text{softmax}\left(\frac{Q_{\text{audio}}K_{\text{visual}}^{\top}}{\sqrt{d_{\text{hidden}}}}\right)V_{\text{visual}} \tag{5.22}$$

- **Cross Attention for Visual Querying Text and Audio Fea-**

tures

1. **Visual Querying Text Features**
   The cross-attention where visual features act as queries to text and audio features is computed in Eq. 5.23 and the cross-attended representation is calculated by Eq. 5.24.

$$Q_{\text{visual}} = W_Q A_{\text{visual}}, K_{\text{text}} = W_K A_{\text{text}}, V_{\text{text}} = W_V A_{\text{text}} \tag{5.23}$$

$$A_{\text{cross,visual}\to\text{text}} = \text{softmax}\left(\frac{Q_{\text{visual}} K_{\text{text}}^{\top}}{\sqrt{d_{\text{hidden}}}}\right) V_{\text{text}} \tag{5.24}$$

2. **Visual Querying Audio Features**
   Similarly, visual features querying audio features is computed using Eq. 5.25. The cross-attended representation is achieved using Eq. 5.26.

$$K_{\text{audio}} = W_K A_{\text{audio}}, V_{\text{audio}} = W_V A_{\text{audio}} \tag{5.25}$$

$$A_{\text{cross,visual}\to\text{audio}} = \text{softmax}\left(\frac{Q_{\text{visual}} K_{\text{audio}}^{\top}}{\sqrt{d_{\text{hidden}}}}\right) V_{\text{audio}} \tag{5.26}$$

5.2.3 Feature Fusion

- **Concatenation of Attended Features**
  The attended features, which are the cross-attention of text, audio and visual respectively, are combined using Eq.5.27.

$$\begin{aligned} Z_{\text{combined}} = \text{concat}(&A_{\text{cross,text}\to\text{visual}}, A_{\text{cross,text}\to\text{audio}}, \\ &A_{\text{cross,visual}\to\text{text}}, A_{\text{cross,visual}\to\text{audio}}, \\ &A_{\text{cross,audio}\to\text{text}}, A_{\text{cross,audio}\to\text{visual}}) \end{aligned} \tag{5.27}$$

  here, $Z_{combined}$ is represented as combined features.

- **Fully Connected Layer** The fully connected layer is used to transform the combined features into the final fused representation as shown in Eq. 5.28.

$$Z_{\text{fused}} = W_{\text{fc}} Z_{\text{combined}} \tag{5.28}$$

In this context, W_{fc} is the weight matrix of the fully connected layer, which maps the combined feature space to lower dimensions. Z_{fused} is the fused feature representation, which the classifier receives from the fully connected layer. In addition, the final fused features are passed for classification for sentiment prediction. The complete process is explained with the help of the Algorithm 2 is given below.

Algorithm 2 Hierarchical Attention-Based Fusion (HABF)

Input: Text features X'_{text}, Audio features X'_{audio}, Visual features X'_{visual}
Output: Predicted sentiment y
Step 1: Self-Attention
foreach *modality* $X' \in \{X'_{text}, X'_{audio}, X'_{visual}\}$ **do**
  Project features into hidden space: $H = W_{\text{proj}} X'$
  Compute Q, K, V matrices:
  $Q = W_Q H, \quad K = W_K H, \quad V = W_V H$
  Compute self-attention:
  $A_{\text{self}} = \text{softmax}\left(\frac{QK^\top}{\sqrt{d_{\text{hidden}}}}\right) V$
end
Step 2: Cross-Attention
foreach *querying modality* $Q \in \{A_{text}, A_{audio}, A_{visual}\}$ **do**
  foreach *attended modality* $K, V \in \{A_{text}, A_{audio}, A_{visual}\}$, *where* $K \neq Q$ **do**
    Compute cross-attention:
    $A_{\text{cross, query}\to\text{attended}} = \text{softmax}\left(\frac{Q_{\text{query}} K^\top_{\text{attended}}}{\sqrt{d_{\text{hidden}}}}\right) V_{\text{attended}}$
  end
end
Step 3: Aggregate features
$Z_{\text{combined}} = \text{concat}(A_{\text{cross,text}\to\text{visual}}, A_{\text{cross,text}\to\text{audio}},$
$A_{\text{cross,visual}\to\text{text}}, A_{\text{cross,visual}\to\text{audio}},$
$A_{\text{cross,audio}\to\text{text}}, A_{\text{cross,audio}\to\text{visual}})$
Step 4: Feature Fusion
Combine fused outputs:
$Z_{\text{fused}} = W_{\text{fc}} Z_{\text{combined}}$
Step 5: Classification
Pass Z_{fused} to classifier:
$y = \text{Classifier}(Z_{\text{fused}})$
Return sentiment label as positive, negative or neutral.

5.3 Classification

The selected features are passed for classification to identify the sentiments. The detailed is discussed in Chapter 3 Section 3.4. The weighted soft voting performs better in classifying sentiments.

5.4 Experimental Setup

This section begins with an overview of the specifics and preparation of the benchmark datasets that will be used to assess our model. Then a summary of the baseline models used is provided. Subsequently, an explanation of the experimental details and experiments that are implemented is provided.

5.4.1 Dataset Description

Experiments were conducted using two datasets: one with the Customer-Generated Sentiment Videos (CGSV) specifically curated for MSA in the restaurant review domain and the other with the published dataset, CMU-MOSI [102]. The CGSV dataset comprises video reviews collected from individuals who give their opinions on restaurant experiences. Today, before visiting any restaurant, people search online for reviews and then visit the corresponding restaurant. Due to the usage of smartphones and the Internet, the posting of reviews in different forms has increased tremendously, one of which is video. This dataset captures the complexities of customer feedback, offering researchers the opportunity to develop and evaluate advanced multimodal fusion techniques that can integrate text, audio and visual modalities in real-world applications.

In order to provide the practical application of the proposed model, 93 videos of well-known restaurants were created that are highly regarded dining establishments and favored by both Indian and international visitors. All participants provided informed consent, and the data were anonymized by avoiding the collection of personal identifiers and ensuring that the videos contained no identifiable information.

A team of three domain experts specializing in human behavior assessment and SA manually annotated the video dataset. Sentiment labels (positive, negative and neutral) were assigned to the overall video based on the analysis of text, audio and visual cues. The transcript content was evaluated for sentiment-laden words and phrases, while audio features such as tone, pitch, energy and speech rate were analyzed for emotional context. Visual features, including facial expressions (e.g. smiling, frowning) and gestures (e.g. nodding, shaking), were also considered. The annotation process ensured alignment across modalities, prioritizing the dominant cues when conflicts occurred. For example, if text and audio conveyed negativity, while visual cues were neutral, the sentiment label reflected the consensus of text and audio.

There are a total of 93 videos, of which 45 positive, 30 negative and 18 neutral videos. Analyzing and identifying the consumer sentiment in these data is crucial as it provides restaurant administrators with valuable insight for improvement. Figure 5.4 shows snapshots of video samples from our dataset.

Figure 5.4: Snapshots of Videos from Dataset CGSV

The details of the dataset are presented in Table 3.5. After applying the suggested methodology to the dataset, several significant experimental outcomes are displayed.

Table 5.1: Dataset Details

Parameters	Value
Total number of videos	93
Number of unique speakers	54
Average video duration	10–12 sec
Average number of extracted frames	1000+
Average word count per transcript	20

The second dataset that we use is the standard named CMU-MOSI. It consists of 93 opinion videos included in the collection involving 86 distinct speakers. It has textual, visual and audio details, making it suitable for analyzing MSA. Thus, the use of both a real-world CGSV dataset and the benchmark CMU-MOSI dataset ensures practical relevance and experimental credibility. This combination enables robust evaluation of multimodal sentiment fusion in controlled and real-world settings.

a. Extraction of Frames, Audio and Transcript

An output directory is created within both the train and test folders. This directory is organized into three subfolders, each representing one of the sentiment classes (e.g., positive, negative and neutral). Within each class folder, individual subfolders are created for each video, named using the format $video_n$, where n denotes the video index. Each of these video-specific folders contains two subdirectories:

- frames/ – Stores the extracted video frames saved in .jpg format.
- transcript/ – Contains both the extracted audio in .wav format and the corresponding textual transcript in .txt format.

This structured organization facilitates synchronized access to multimodal data components for feature extraction and further analysis.

5.4.2 HABF Experimental Settings

Both datasets are divided into 80% training and 20% testing. The details of the experimental setting of HABF technique are presented in Table 5.2. It includes tuning of parameters for the HABF technique to ensure that they yield sufficient feature representation with superior performance in sentiment prediction across modalities, thus demonstrating the robustness of the HABF technique. The text and image feature extraction parameter setting is the same as discussed earlier. For audio resampling rate of 16 kHz and 29-dimensional (MFCCs, chroma, spectral, RMS and ZCR)-Librosa features).

Table 5.2: Parameters of HABF

Text dimension	256
Image dimension	1512
Audio dimension	29 (Librosa features)
Hidden dimension for attention mechanisms	64 (tuned from 64, 128, 256)
Attention heads	8 (tuned from 2, 4, 8)

The tuned HABF parameters ensure effective cross-modal representation learning while maintaining computational efficiency. This setup highlights the robustness of the proposed fusion strategy across heterogeneous modalities.

5.4.3 Sentiment Categorization Criteria

The suggested model output is classified into three categories: positive (2), negative (0) and neutral (1). Sentiment scores are assigned to each category in the range as shown in Table 5.3.

Table 5.3: Sentiment Categories and Assigned Values

Sentiment Score Range	Assigned Sentiment Category	Description
$0 \leq \text{score} < 1$	Negative	Captures dissatisfaction, criticism, or discontent through harsh text, low-energy tones, or negative visual expressions.
$1 \leq \text{score} < 1.5$	Neutral	Represents balanced or mixed feedback; none of the modalities strongly indicate positive or negative sentiment.
$1.5 \leq \text{score} \leq 2$	Positive	Associated with enthusiastic tones, smiling expressions and positive textual content.

The clear sentiment score thresholds ensure consistent interpretation of multimodal predictions. This improves classification reliability and supports meaningful sentiment analysis of video reviews.

5.5 Result Analysis

In order to demonstrate the effectiveness of the proposed system, an experimental investigation was performed on publicly available CMU-MOSI and custom CGSV datasets. The metrics used to evaluate the performance of a model include P, R, Acc and F1. For a more thorough analysis, the Corr and MAE were also calculated.

The comparison of the accuracy between different classifiers and fusion techniques in the CGSV dataset is shown in Table 5.4 and Table 5.5. The features are extracted from text using BiLSTM, visual using CNN and audio using librosa. To these features, different fusion techniques are applied. Early fusion simply concatenates the extracted features and passes them on to the various classifiers. Late Fusion processes each modality independently through its dedicated classifier and then combines the individual predictions to derive a final sentiment decision. Our fusion technique (HABF) outperforms with the weighted soft voting ensemble classifier and achieves an accuracy of 80.24%.

Table 5.4: Classifier Performance under Different Fusion Strategies using Features Extracted via BiLSTM (text), CNN (visual) and Librosa (audio).

Classifier	**Fusion Technique**	**Acc**	**P**	**R**	**F1**
SVM	Early	76.42	75.30	75.80	75.50
	Late	74.08	73.50	73.90	73.70
	HABF	78.10	77.40	77.90	76.90
NB	Early	68.50	67.20	66.00	66.60
	Late	66.90	65.70	64.80	65.20
	HABF	70.60	69.50	69.00	70.00
KNN	Early	70.20	68.50	68.90	68.70
	Late	68.70	67.00	66.50	66.70
	HABF	72.80	71.00	71.50	70.80

Table 5.5: Classifier Performance under Different Fusion Strategies using Features Extracted via BiLSTM (text), CNN (visual) and Librosa (audio) (Continued).

Classifier	**Fusion Technique**	**Acc**	**P**	**R**	**F1**
LR	Early	72.10	70.60	70.90	70.70
	Late	70.30	69.00	68.50	68.70
	HABF	74.20	73.80	73.60	73.00
DF	Early	69.80	68.40	68.70	68.50
	Late	67.40	66.00	65.20	65.60
	HABF	71.90	70.60	71.10	70.00
Soft Voting	Early	74.50	73.20	73.60	73.40
	Late	72.80	71.00	70.50	70.70
	HABF	75.80	74.00	74.60	74.30
Hard Voting	Early	74.30	73.00	73.30	73.10
	Late	72.40	70.80	70.20	70.50
	HABF	76.10	75.00	75.20	75.10
Bagging	Early	75.20	74.10	74.50	74.30
	Late	73.10	72.00	71.40	71.70
	HABF	76.20	75.60	75.80	75.90
AdaBoost	Early	75.10	74.00	74.20	74.10
	Late	73.00	71.90	71.30	71.60
	HABF	77.00	76.20	76.50	76.60
Gradient Boosting	Early	75.60	74.30	74.70	74.50
	Late	73.40	72.50	71.90	72.20
	HABF	77.30	76.80	77.10	77.20
Stacking	Early	75.80	74.60	75.00	74.80
	Late	73.70	72.80	72.10	72.50
	HABF	78.00	77.60	78.10	78.00
Weighted Soft Voting	Early	78.20	77.00	77.40	77.20
	Late	76.20	75.00	74.60	74.80
	HABF	80.24	79.80	80.00	80.10

Similarly, a comparison of the accuracy between various classifiers and fusion techniques was made in the CGSV dataset, where the features are extracted from text using BERT-iBiLSTM, visual using WaveNet-CNN and audio using librosa. The fused features were passed to different ML classifiers (SVM, NB, KNN, LR, DF and ensemble), and the results obtained from the experiments offer a comprehensive comparison as shown in Table 5.6 and Table 5.7.

The results indicate that the proposed feature extraction method yields an accuracy improvement of about 1%.

Table 5.6: Classifier Performance with Different Fusion Strategies using BERT-iBiLSTM (text), WaveNet-CNN (visual) and Librosa (audio)

Classifier	Fusion Technique	Acc	P	R	F1
SVM	Early	76.12	75.12	75.88	75.49
	Late	74.85	74.05	73.55	73.78
	HABF	80.12	79.40	80.80	79.20
NB	Early	69.72	68.34	67.70	67.95
	Late	68.91	67.80	66.95	67.34
	HABF	72.34	71.80	70.30	72.50
KNN	Early	71.75	70.35	69.88	70.07
	Late	70.60	69.42	68.55	69.00
	HABF	74.89	74.50	75.00	73.80
LR	Early	73.62	72.20	71.65	71.88
	Late	72.88	71.65	70.78	71.21
	HABF	76.50	75.90	76.20	75.30
DF	Early	71.42	70.70	69.90	70.29
	Late	70.75	69.95	69.00	69.45
	HABF	73.78	72.90	71.62	74.00
Soft Voting	Early	73.84	71.60	71.25	71.42
	Late	72.30	70.10	70.45	70.30
	HABF	75.62	73.84	74.32	73.89
Hard Voting	Early	74.10	72.45	72.10	72.24
	Late	72.92	71.12	71.25	71.18
	HABF	76.34	74.56	75.14	74.80
Bagging	Early	75.45	73.55	73.00	73.20
	Late	73.87	72.15	72.10	72.00
	HABF	77.50	75.80	76.40	75.90

Table 5.7: Classifier Performance with Different Fusion Strategies using BERT-iBiLSTM (text), WaveNet-CNN (visual) and Librosa (audio) (Continued)

AdaBoost	Early	76.05	74.65	73.78	74.10
	Late	74.76	73.40	73.00	73.55
	HABF	78.20	76.30	77.20	76.90
Gradient Boosting	Early	76.98	75.35	74.88	75.30
	Late	75.48	74.65	74.00	74.65
	HABF	79.01	77.25	78.45	77.80
Stacking	Early	77.45	76.40	75.40	76.20
	Late	76.22	75.22	74.25	75.40
	HABF	80.00	78.90	79.10	78.80
Weighted Soft Voting	Early	78.04	77.12	76.55	77.02
	Late	76.88	76.00	75.60	76.30
	HABF	81.12	79.90	81.20	79.60

The performance comparison of different classifiers in the CMU-MOSI dataset with features extracted from text- BERT-iBiLSTM, visual-WaveNet-CNN and audio-Librosa and using HABF to fuse features is presented in Table 5.8. The various classifiers were tested using different evaluation metrics. KNN was known as the best among individual classifiers, with an Acc of 81.67, an F1 score of 81.76 and a Corr of 0.76. Similarly, good results were obtained for SVM: an accuracy of 78.33 and an F1 score of 78.44. In contrast, NB had the worst performance: only 53.33% in accuracy and 0.63 in MAE, the highest, indicating that it did not generalize well on the data set. LR and DF showed moderate results with an accuracy of around 70-71%. However, the weighted soft voting ensemble outclassed every classifier with an Acc of 87.33%, a P of 87.61% and an R of 87.33% and an F1 of 87.38. It also stands out among all with the lowest MAE (0.18) and the highest Corr score of (0.82), making it superior in multimodal sentiment classification tasks.

Table 5.8: Performance Comparison of Classifiers on CMU-MOSI Dataset.

Classifier	Acc	P	R	F1	MAE	Corr
SVM	78.33	78.84	78.33	78.44	0.27	0.74
NB	53.33	54.26	53.33	51.74	0.63	0.37
KNN	81.67	82.41	81.67	81.76	0.23	0.76
LR	70.67	71.76	70.67	70.88	0.35	0.66
DF	71.00	72.26	71.00	71.23	0.37	0.62
Weighted Soft Voting	87.33	87.61	87.33	87.38	0.18	0.82

The performance comparison of different classifiers in the CSGV dataset which gives the MAE score of 0.16 and the Corr of 0.76 using the proposed system is presented in Table 5.9.

Table 5.9: Performance Comparison of Classifiers on CSGV Dataset.

Classifier	Acc	P	R	F1	MAE	Corr
SVM	80.12	79.40	80.80	79.20	0.18	0.85
NB	72.34	71.80	70.30	72.50	0.24	0.71
KNN	74.89	74.50	75.00	73.80	0.22	0.75
LR	76.50	75.90	76.20	75.30	0.21	0.78
DF	73.78	72.90	71.62	74.00	0.23	0.72
Weighted Soft Voting	81.12	79.90	81.20	79.60	0.16	0.76

The proposed system outperforms all baseline models in any metric with which it is tested is shown in Table 5.10. More specifically, it scores the highest maximum Acc of 87.33% on the CMU-MOSI dataset, significantly surpassing models such as UEFN (82.30%) and RMA (82.13%). The P is 87.61% and the R is 87.33%, which indicates that it has a balanced ability to distinguish sentiment classes with a minimal number of false positives and false negatives. Meanwhile, F1 of 87. 38% is reflective of the overall ability of the model to handle P, R trade-offs. BiLSTM-MA combines bidirectional LSTM and multiple attention mechanisms to achieve an Acc of 81.50% in classification and an F1 of 79.10%. The BiLSTM with Attention model would further raise this performance using improved attention methods, with Acc recorded as high as 80.18%. Further substantiation shows that the proposed model achieves an impressively low MAE of 0.180, including a high Corr of 0.880, indicating both Acc in sentiment predictions and negligible errors. HABF is the most statistically significant proven model for capturing deep interdependencies and dynamically prioritizing important features between modalities. It sets a new standard for MSA performance.

Table 5.10: Performance Comparison of Existing Models with the Proposed Method

Model	**Acc**	**P**	**R**	**F1**
BC-LSTM [103]	74.60	75.33	74.43	74.50
GME-LSTM(A) [104]	75.70	72.20	73.30	73.90
TFN [108]	76.40	75.30	74.20	74.80
MARN [105]	77.10	75.80	74.60	77.80
MFN [106]	77.40	75.80	74.60	75.20
BiLSTM with Attention Model [76]	81.30	80.20	79.10	79.60
ULMD [83]	81.42	79.50	78.99	79.11
Bi-LSTM(MA) [85]	81.50	79.69	78.50	79.12
MAMSA [84]	81.83	79.36	79.00	81.80
SKEAFN [107]	82.10	81.00	79.90	80.40
RMA [82]	82.13	80.24	79.36	80.50
UEFN [80]	82.30	80.47	79.18	80.78
MISA [112]	83.60	83.10	83.50	83.20
ATMGT [113]	84.08	83.50	84.10	83.70
MAG-BERT [114]	84.50	84.20	84.60	84.30
Proposed Model(HABF)	87.33	87.61	87.33	87.38

The evaluation of the generalization of the proposed model is shown in Table 5.11. The experiments were performed with training on the CMU-MOSI dataset and testing the CGSV dataset, or training CGSV and testing on CMU-MOSI. BERT-iBiLSTM, WaveNet-CNN and Librosa extracted the modalities of Text (T), Visual (V) and Audio (A), respectively, and fed them to a weighted soft voting ensemble classifier that demonstrated superior performance in classification. We followed the same procedure for modality combinations such as T+A, T+V, A+V and T+A+V. The obtained features are fused using HABF to effectively capture inter-modal relationships and then passed the fused features to the classifier for final sentiment classification. The results clearly show that some modalities, in contrast to single modalities, improve generalization performance. It confirms that the use of all three modalities (T+A+V) will give the best results. This shows that HABF works to resolve conflicting signals and improve sentiment classification performance across datasets.

Table 5.11: Cross-Dataset Performance for Different Modality Combinations

Modality Combination	CMU-MOSI → CGSV	CGSV → CMU-MOSI
T (Text)	60.27	48.34
V (Video)	49.16	43.21
A (Audio)	48.73	42.67
T + A	64.81	52.58
T + V	66.43	54.22
A + V	61.27	51.34
T + A + V	69.95	56.83

5.5.1 Case Study: Conflict Resolution

Consider a video that presents a customer sharing a review about a restaurant experience, where both verbal content and facial expressions are visible. Although spoken words convey the customer's opinion, accompanying expressions such as smiles, frowns, or neutral looks provide additional sentimental signals. Further details are given below.

Transcript: "The food is really fantastic and the ambiance is very good".

Visual Expression: The subject maintains his face with minimal gestures, not smiling, or appears uninterested lacking congruent excitement or engagement.

Audio Tone: Spoken in a calm and flat tone, lacking emotional intensity or pitch variation typically associated with happiness.

It presents a more challenging scenario with conflicting modalities. The transcript carried a positive sentiment with a score of 1.5328, indicating strong satisfaction with its textual content. However, according to the visual modality in frame analysis, dissatisfaction or at best non-expression was reflected in the opposition with a score of 0.9491. Meanwhile, by the audio modality on tone and prosody, the delivery was calm and neutral; therefore, it had a sentiment score of 1.2119. While inter-modally different with positive being text, negative being visuals and neutral being audio, the HABF model smartly intercepts these inputs. Hence, it follows the majority voice of the text, aided by the other modalities. With this, the final multimodal sentiment score fell to neutral at 1.2132, according to the defining threshold scale.

The output of the same is shown in Figure 5.5. This synergizes well with the overall affective manifestation of the video, which, although textually positive, lacks visual and audio emotional intensity. This case study demonstrates the robustness of the HABF model in handling conflicting sentiment cues across modalities. It validates the model's capability to weigh modalities contextually, ensuring an accurate and coherent final sentiment prediction that closely reflects the true emotional tone of the video.

For Transcript:

```
# ==============================
# MAIN
# ==============================
if __name__ == "__main__":
    txt_input_path = "/Users/[illegible]/Desktop/multimodalproject/FinalModel/output/test/test3/transcript/transcript.txt"
    predict_sentiment_from_txt(txt_input_path)

MoviePy - Writing audio in testfolder/transcript/audio.wav

MoviePy - Done.

Sentiment score: 1.5328
Predicted Sentiment: Positive
```

For Frames:

```
✅ Final averaged feature shape: (1, 1512)
Sentiment Score: 0.9491
Predicted Sentiment: Negative
```

For audio:

```
if __name__ == "__main__":
    wav_input_path = "/Users/[illegible]/Desktop/multimodalproject/FinalModel/output/test/test3/transcript/audio.wav"
    predict_sentiment_from_wav(wav_input_path)

Sentiment Score: 1.2119
Predicted Sentiment: Neutral
```

After Fusion:

```
MoviePy - Writing audio in testfolder/transcript/audio.wav

MoviePy - Done.

Video Sentiment score: 1.2132
Video Predicted Sentiment: Neutral
```

Figure 5.5: Output of Conflict Resolution

The attention heatmap which shows how the HABF model resolves conflicting sentiment cues across modalities to arrive at a final neutral prediction is illustrated in Figure 5.6. Although the text modality exhibited a strong positive sentiment score (1.5328), both audio (1.2119) and visual (0.9491) conveyed neutral to slightly negative cues. The attention weights show that while text receives the highest self-attention (0.41), significant attention is still paid to audio and visual cues (0.33 and 0.26, respectively). Audio, with a neutral tone, contributes heavily due to its self-attention (0.40) and visual features receive moderate attention while presenting a negative signal. This balanced attention across modalities prevents the model from being biased by highly positive textual content. As a result, HABF integrates these inputs and outputs a sentiment score of 1.2132, which accurately falls into the neutral category. This showcases HABF's capability to manage intermodal conflicts and derive context-aware sentiment interpretations.

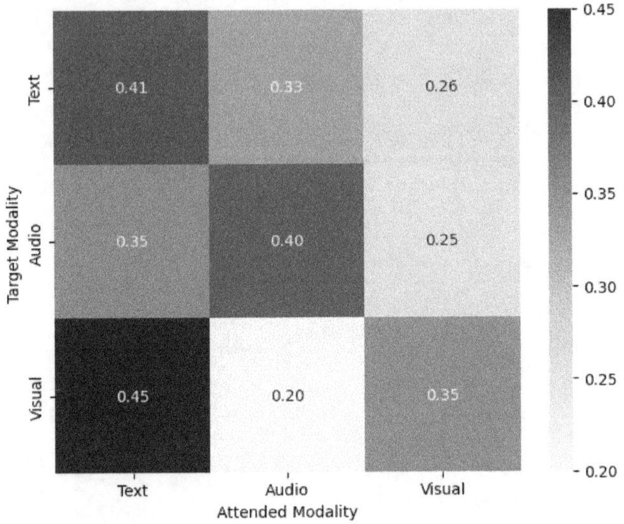

Figure 5.6: Attention Heatmap for HABF Conflict Resolution

5.6 Findings

This section presents sample results obtained from the implementation of the proposed video SA system. The outputs shown are screenshots captured directly from the code execution environment, showcasing the system's performance in analyzing and classifying sentiment from video inputs. Each result demonstrates the sentiment prediction process based on the fusion of features extracted from text (transcripts), audio (tone and pitch) and visual (facial expressions and gestures) modalities into categories such as positive, negative and neutral.

Figure 5.7 shows the sentiment classification result for negative video.

```
video_path = "/Users/Desktop/multimodalproject/FinalModel/test/test1_negative.mp4"
if __name__ == "__main__":
    score = predict_video(video_path)
    if score is not None:
        print(f"Sentiment score: {score:.4f}")
```

```
MoviePy - Writing audio in testfolder/transcript/audio.wav

MoviePy - Done.

Sentiment score: 0.8631
Predicted Sentiment: Negative
```

Figure 5.7: Sentiment Classification Result for Negative Video

Figure 5.8 shows the sentiment classification result for neutral video.

```
video_path = "/Users/Desktop/multimodalproject/FinalModel/test/test2_neutral.mp4"
if __name__ == "__main__":
    score = predict_video(video_path)
    if score is not None:
        print(f"Sentiment score: {score:.4f}")
```

```
MoviePy - Writing audio in testfolder/transcript/audio.wav

MoviePy - Done.

Sentiment score: 1.4532
Predicted Sentiment: Neutral
```

Figure 5.8: Sentiment Classification Result for a Neutral Video

Figures 5.9 shows the sentiment classification result for positive video.

VIDEO: Positive

```
video_path = "/Users/Desktop/multimodalproject/FinalModel/test/test6_positive.mp4"
if __name__ == "__main__":
    score = predict_video(video_path)
    if score is not None:
        print(f"Sentiment score: {score:.4f}")
        if 0 <= score < 1:
            sentiment = "Negative"
```

```
MoviePy - Writing audio in testfolder/transcript/audio.wav

MoviePy - Done.

Sentiment score: 1.5328
Predicted Sentiment: Positive
```

Figure 5.9: Sentiment Classification Result for a Positive Video

The visual outputs discussed above validate the practical functionality and effectiveness of the proposed system in handling real-world video reviews, supporting and visually strengthening the quantitative performance results.

5.7 Summary

Videos inherently combine textual, audio, and visual modalities, making SA challenging due to the need for effective integration of diverse features. In addition, most researchers used general purpose datasets, and hence there is a need for a domain-specific dataset. In light of these considerations, the CGSV dataset is developed which consists of video clips of restaurant reviews. A novel HABF method is proposed for integrating features from text, audio and visual modalities using self- and cross-attention mechanisms in a hierarchical manner. It dynamically resolves conflicts between modalities and highlights the most important features for sentiment classification. Several experimental evaluations were performed on the CGSV and CMU-MOSI datasets. The experiments carried out show that the accuracy: 87.33% and 81.12% for the CMU-MOSI and CGSV datasets, respectively. To demonstrate the superiority of the proposed model, its performance was compared with that of baseline models using the CMU-MOSI dataset. Further cross-dataset experiments were performed, in which the system was trained on the CMU-MOSI dataset and tested on the CGSV dataset, and vice versa to demonstrate the generalization ability of the model. The model outperforms traditional early and late fusion techniques in various datasets, achieving state-of-the-art accuracies. This system is able to analyze video reviews in practical scenarios, such as customer feedback in the restaurant and hospitality industries, to provide the information necessary for improved service and experience.

In next chapter, an integrated sentiment analysis model using multimodal input (text, image and video) will be discussed.

Chapter 6

Contribution 4: An Integrated Sentiment Analysis Model using Multimodal Inputs (Text, Image and Video)

Users express their sentiments through text, images and videos, across various digital platforms, sentiment analysis methods that are traditionally unimodal cannot capture the entire emotional context. To this end, a combined sentiment analysis system should be built that accepts any form of multimodal input for analysis, individually, or in combination. This will provide a much stronger ability to predict sentiments in real and flexible contexts.

This chapter shows the proposed integrated sentiment analysis model that is able to predict sentiments for multimodal inputs, i.e. text (T), images (I) and videos (V) individually, or in combination, like (text + image (T+I), text + video (T+V), image + video (I+V) and text + image + video (T+I+V)). The different modalities are processed through their corresponding unimodal pipeline and late fusion is applied that integrates the individual predictions. The architecture of the proposed model is illustrated in Figure 6.1.

The following sections describe the integration process for the proposed novel sentiment analysis model. Section 6.1 provides for the derivation of late fusion using a weighted aggregation approach by which predictions from multiple modalities are combined to produce a single sentiment score. The formulation also allows the system to account for the relative reliability and contribution of each modality. Section 6.2 discusses a concrete example of computing a unified sentiment prediction from multimodal inputs – text, image and video – using the restaurant review setting to illustrate how each modality's sentiment-relevant information is effectively combined. Finally, Section 6.3 proposes a complete model computation example in the restaurant reviews dataset.

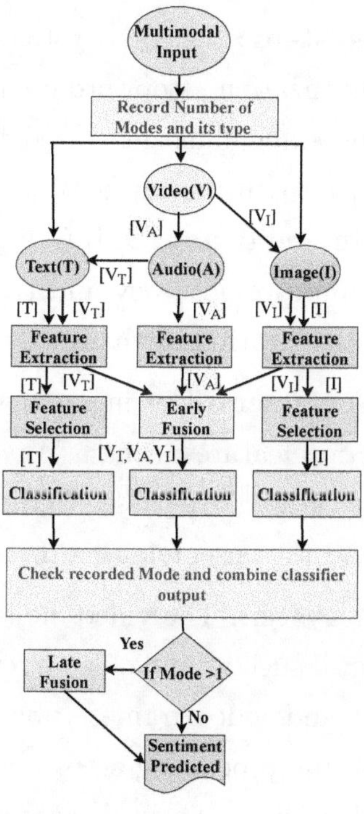

Figure 6.1: Proposed Integrated Model for Sentiment Analysis of Multimodal Inputs

A detailed explanation of each step of the system is given below.

1. Multimodal Input

    - The system accepts input in different forms: text(T), images(I) and videos(V).

2. Record Number of Modes and Its Type

    - The system records the number of input modes and identifies the types (T, I, V).

3. Processing Individual Modalities

    - **Text SA system :** The text system includes data pre-processing, such as tokenization, stopword removal and converting to lowercase. The embedding generated from BERT was then subsequently fed into an improved BiLSTM technique for feature extraction. In addition, a DMFO algorithm for feature selection is used to improve accuracy and then pass these features to the ensemble classification method.
    - **Image SA sytsem** The image system includes pre-processing and extraction features using a WaveNet-CNN method. Furthermore, these features are passed to the DMFO algorithm for feature selection and the ensemble classification method.
    - **Video SA system** The video file is given as input and multiple forms of data, such as audio (V_A), text (transcript) obtained from audio (V_T) and video frames (images) (V_I) are extracted from it.Then the pre-processing steps and feature extraction methods are applied to them. Then, these features are fused using an early fusion method called HABF. In addition, these resulting features are passed to the ensemble classification method to predict sentiment.

4. Check Recorded Mode and Combine Classifier Output

- The system checks the recorded modes (number and types of input) and prepares to combine the classifier outputs accordingly.

5. Late Fusion

   - **If Mode > 1:**
     - Late Fusion: Combine the outputs of the classifiers from each modality using the weighted aggregation method.
     - Sentiment Predicted: The final sentiment is predicted on the basis of the unified output.
   - **If Mode = 1:**
     - Sentiment Predicted: Directly use the output of the single modality classifier for sentiment prediction.

6.1 Derivation of Late Fusion using Weighted Aggregation

Late fusion integrates the outputs obtained from unimodal models to produce a final sentiment prediction. In the weighted aggregation method, each modality contributes proportionally based on its sentiment score, ensuring adaptive and context-sensitive integration.

6.1.1 Representation of Modalities

The following notations are used to represent sentiment scores, weights, and modality indicators:

- S_t, S_i, S_v be the sentiment scores obtained from the text, image and video modalities, respectively.
- W_t, W_i, W_v be the computed normalized weights for text, image and video, based on their respective sentiment scores.
- $M_t, M_i, M_v \in \{0, 1\}$ be binary variables indicating the presence of each modality:

- $M_t = 1$ if text is available, else 0.
- $M_i = 1$ if image is available, else 0.
- $M_v = 1$ if video is available, else 0.

6.1.2 Computation of Weights

If a modality is present ($M_x = 1$), its score contributes to the total score:

$$S_{\text{total}} = M_t S_t + M_i S_i + M_v S_v$$

The normalized weights are computed as:

$$W_t = \frac{M_t S_t}{S_{\text{total}}}, \quad W_i = \frac{M_i S_i}{S_{\text{total}}}, \quad W_v = \frac{M_v S_v}{S_{\text{total}}}$$

6.1.3 Final Sentiment Score Calculation

The final sentiment score is obtained as shown in Eq. 6.1.

$$S_{\text{final}} = M_t \cdot W_t \cdot S_t + M_i \cdot W_i \cdot S_i + M_v \cdot W_v \cdot S_v \tag{6.1}$$

This approach dynamically adjusts the influence of each modality based on their relative strengths and the availability of scores.

Explanation

- If a modality is absent ($M_x = 0$), its contribution is ignored.

6.1.4 Special Cases for Different Modalities

1. All Three Modalities Present ($M_t = M_i = M_v = 1$) The final equation when all modalities (T, I, V) are present is shown in Eq. 6.2.

$$S_{\text{total}} = S_t + S_i + S_v$$

$$W_t = \frac{S_t}{S_{\text{total}}}, \quad W_i = \frac{S_i}{S_{\text{total}}}, \quad W_v = \frac{S_v}{S_{\text{total}}}$$

$$S_{\text{final}} = W_t S_t + W_i S_i + W_v S_v \tag{6.2}$$

2. Text + Image ($M_t = 1, M_i = 1, M_v = 0$) The final equation when the modalities (T and I) are present is shown in Eq. 6.3.

$$
\begin{gathered}
S_{\text{total}} = S_t + S_i \\
W_t = \frac{S_t}{S_{\text{total}}}, \quad W_i = \frac{S_i}{S_{\text{total}}} \\
S_{\text{final}} = W_t S_t + W_i S_i
\end{gathered} \tag{6.3}
$$

3. Text + Video ($M_t = 1, M_i = 0, M_v = 1$) The final equation when the modalities (T and V) are present is shown in Eq. 6.4.

$$
\begin{gathered}
S_{\text{total}} = S_t + S_v \\
W_t = \frac{S_t}{S_{\text{total}}}, \quad W_v = \frac{S_v}{S_{\text{total}}} \\
S_{\text{final}} = W_t S_t + W_v S_v
\end{gathered} \tag{6.4}
$$

4. Image + Video ($M_t = 0, M_i = 1, M_v = 1$) The final equation when the modalities (I and V) are present is shown in Eq. 6.5.

$$
\begin{gathered}
S_{\text{total}} = S_i + S_v \\
W_i = \frac{S_i}{S_{\text{total}}}, \quad W_v = \frac{S_v}{S_{\text{total}}} \\
S_{\text{final}} = W_i S_i + W_v S_v
\end{gathered} \tag{6.5}
$$

5. Only One Modality Present (Unimodal Fusion) The final equation when either of the modalities (T, I or V) is present is shown in Eqs. 6.6, 6.7, 6.8.

(a) **Text Present** ($M_t = 1, M_i = 0, M_v = 0$)

$$
S_{\text{final}} = S_t \tag{6.6}
$$

(b) **Image Present** $(M_t = 0, M_i = 1, M_v = 0)$

$$S_{\text{final}} = S_i \tag{6.7}$$

(c) **Video Present** $(M_t = 0, M_i = 0, M_v = 1)$

$$S_{\text{final}} = S_v \tag{6.8}$$

This formulation ensures that each available modality contributes proportionally to the final sentiment score based on its individual relevance while gracefully degrading in the absence of any modality.

6.2 System Setup and Hardware Configuration

The proposed framework relies on open-source deep learning libraries and publicly available datasets, minimizing licensing costs. Resource requirements mainly involve GPU-based training for deep models. Deployment cost considerations depend on scale and infrastructure and were not explicitly analyzed, as the thesis emphasizes model design and performance validation rather than economic feasibility analysis.

Hardware Requirement and System setup

- All experiments were conducted using Google Colab with GPU acceleration.
- The computational environment included an Intel Core i5 processor operating at 2.5 GHz.
- The system was equipped with 24 GB of RAM.
- NVIDIA GPU support was utilized to accelerate model training and inference.
- A storage capacity of 1 TB was used for dataset management.

This configuration was sufficient to support the training and evaluation of deep learning models, multimodal feature fusion, and ensemble classification.

6.3 Real-World Validation

In a real-world deployment scenario, a restaurant typically receives multiple user reviews in different modalities. To simulate this setting, a total of 80 reviews were considered for a single restaurant, comprising 50 text reviews, 20 image reviews, and 10 video reviews. The proposed system does not generate 80 independent final outputs. Instead, it follows a hierarchical output structure that culminates in a single integrated sentiment decision.

At the first level, each review is processed independently by its corresponding modality-specific model. This results in internal sentiment scores that are used exclusively for aggregation and are not directly presented to end-users.

For the text modality, 50 sentiment scores are produced:

$$T_1 = 1.82,\ T_2 = 1.91,\ \ldots,\ T_{50} = 1.76$$

Similarly, the image and video subsystems generate 20 and 10 sentiment scores each respectively:

$$I_1 = 1.12,\ I_2 = 1.18,\ \ldots,\ I_{20} = 1.09$$

$$V_1 = 1.01,\ V_2 = 1.07,\ \ldots,\ V_{10} = 1.04$$

In total, 80 individual sentiment predictions are generated internally at this stage.

To prevent bias caused by unequal review counts across modalities, the system aggregates predictions at the modality level. Each modality produces a single representative sentiment score computed as the mean of its individual predictions.

$$S_{\text{t}} = \frac{1}{50} \sum_{i=1}^{50} T_i = 1.83 \text{ (Positive)}$$

$$S_{\text{i}} = \frac{1}{10} \sum_{i=1}^{20} I_i = 1.15 \text{ (Neutral)}$$

$$S_{\text{v}} = \frac{1}{10} \sum_{i=1}^{10} V_i = 1.04 \text{ (Neutral)}$$

At this stage, the system retains exactly three modality-level scores:

$$\{S_{\text{t}} = 1.83,\ S_{\text{i}} = 1.15,\ S_{\text{v}} = 1.04\}$$

The modality-level scores are integrated using an adaptive weighted aggregation strategy. Each modality is assigned a weight proportional to its sentiment confidence score, ensuring balanced contribution across modalities.

The normalized weight for each modality is computed as:

$$W_t = \frac{S_t}{S_{\text{total}}}, \quad W_i = \frac{S_i}{S_{\text{total}}}, \quad W_v = \frac{S_v}{S_{\text{total}}}$$

The sum of modality scores is:

$$\sum S_{\text{total}} = 1.83 + 1.15 + 1.04 = 4.02$$

Thus, the weights are:

$$W_{\text{t}} = \frac{1.83}{4.02} = 0.455$$

$$W_{\text{i}} = \frac{1.15}{4.02} = 0.286$$

$$W_{\text{v}} = \frac{1.04}{4.02} = 0.259$$

The final fused sentiment score is calculated as:

$$S_{\text{final}} = W_t S_t + W_i S_i + W_v S_v$$

$$S_{\text{final}} = (0.455 \times 1.83) + (0.286 \times 1.15) + (0.259 \times 1.04)$$

$$S_{\text{final}} = 1.431$$

Based on predefined decision thresholds, the final sentiment score is mapped to a sentiment label and star rating.

$$1.0 \leq S_{\text{final}} < 1.5 \Rightarrow \text{Neutral}$$

Accordingly, the final rating is:

$$\text{Overall Rating} = \quad (3 \text{ out of } 5)$$

This single sentiment label and rating represent the overall customer perception of the restaurant and correspond to the output format commonly used by platforms such as Google Reviews, Yelp, and TripAdvisor.

6.3.1 Samples of Unified Sentiment from Multimodal Inputs (Text, Image and Video) in Restaurant Reviews

To generate a unified sentiment output for a particular restaurant, the proposed system processes reviews submitted by different users in various formats: text, image and video. For instance, consider a scenario where three users each provide feedback: one writes a textual review, another uploads an image and the third shares a video. The system first processes each input through its respective unimodal sentiment analysis pipeline text, image and video. Each modality independently generates a sentiment score. These individual scores are then passed to the weighted aggregation module, where the final sentiment score for the restaurant is computed using Eq. 6.2. This score reflects a holistic sentiment by proportionally integrating the insights from all available modalities, ensuring a more accurate and representative sentiment classification.

Text Review:

The food, ambiance and staff are really good, specially Shayak and his team. We stayed for 3 nights and every single meal was exceptional.

Image Review:

Video Review:

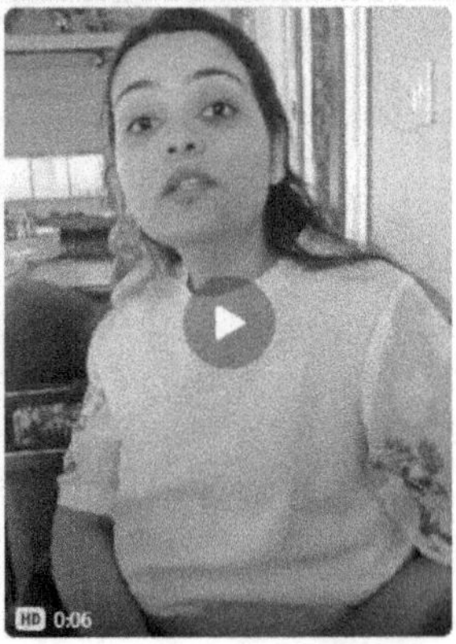


```
Text Sentiment score: 1.8948
Text Predicted Sentiment: Positive
Image Sentiment score: 1.1603
Image Predicted Sentiment: Neutral
MoviePy - Writing audio in testfolder/transcript/audio.wav

MoviePy - Done.

Video Sentiment score: 1.0146
Video Predicted Sentiment: Neutral
MoviePy - Writing audio in testfolder/transcript/audio.wav

MoviePy - Done.

--------------------------------------------------
Modality activation (binary): {'text': 1, 'image': 1, 'video': 1}
--------------------------------------------------
Individual predictions: {'text': 1.8948371445324, 'image': 1.1603435083532072, 'video': 1.0549452218023414}
--------------------------------------------------
Fusion Results:
--------------------------------------------------
Simple Aggregation: 1.3700
--------------------------------------------------
Weighted Aggregation: 1.4719
--------------------------------------------------
Simple Aggregation Sentiment Score: 1.3700
Predicted Sentiment: Neutral
--------------------------------------------------
Weighted Aggregation Sentiment Score: 1.4719
Predicted Sentiment: Neutral
--------------------------------------------------
☆ Star Rating: ☆☆☆ (3 out of 5)
--------------------------------------------------
```

Figure 6.2: Output of the Proposed Sentiment Analysis Model using multimodal inputs, Showing Individual Modality Scores, Predicted Sentiments and Final Sentiment via Fusion Techniques

Figure 6.2 shows the output of a multimodal sentiment analysis system that takes into account reviews offered by clients in text, image and video formats for a restaurant. The text review is positive (score: 1.8948), the image is neutral (score: 1.1603) and the video is negative (score: 1.0146).

The binary activations signify all three modalities as active. Sentiments are independently predicted for each modality by the respective corresponding unimodal models. Then, two final aggregations for sentiment calculation are applied: simple average and weighted aggregation. In simple aggregation, each of the scores is given equal weight in the average; thus, the final sentiment has been calculated to be 1.3799.

According to weighted aggregation, scores of each modality are weighted according to their proportions in the total score, with 1.4767 being the final number. Both fusion approaches result in a prediction for the overall sentiment, in which the system balances the differing sentiments between modalities. In particular, if only textual reviews were considered, the system would have predicted a positive sentiment, which would not reflect the true overall opinion of the users. This highlights the importance of integrating image and video data to capture a more accurate and holistic view of user sentiment. Finally, the rating is calculated on the basis of the range discussed in the following Table 6.1.

Table 6.1: Score Range to Star Rating Mapping

Score Range	**Star Rating**	**Visual Representation**
$0 \leq \text{score} < 0.5$	1 Star	☆
$0.5 \leq \text{score} \leq 0.9$	2 Stars	☆ ☆
$1 \leq \text{score} < 1.5$	3 Stars	☆ ☆ ☆
$1.5 \leq \text{score} < 1.7$	4 Stars	☆ ☆ ☆ ☆
$1.7 \leq \text{score} \leq 2$	5 Stars	☆ ☆ ☆ ☆ ☆
score > 2 or invalid	0 Star	-

6.4 Proposed Model on Restaurant Reviews Dataset

This explains the results of late fusion using both weighted aggregation and simple aggregation.

6.4.1 Using Weighted Aggregation

For the proposed model, the accuracy is used for the calculation of the restaurant domain-related reviews dataset. For text (Dataset 3: Restaurant reviews), from image (Dataset 3: Restaurant review images) and for video the Customer-Generated Sentiment Videos (CGSV) is used. Here, A_t, A_i, A_v be the accuracies of the text, image and video classifiers, respectively.

- **One Modality Present**

  When only a single modality is available, the system directly reports the accuracy obtained from the corresponding classifier:

  - Text-only Accuracy: $A_t = 98.77\%$
  - Image-only Accuracy: $A_i = 89.72\%$
  - Video-only Accuracy: $A_v = 81.12\%$

  These results indicate that textual information provides the most discriminative cues for restaurant sentiment analysis.

- **Two Modality Present**

  When two modalities are available, weighted aggregation is applied.

  - **Text + Image Fusion**

$$A_{\text{total}} = A_t + A_i = 0.9877 + 0.8972 = 1.8849$$

$$A_{\text{final}}^{(T+I)} = 94.50\%$$

  - **Text + Video Fusion**

$$A_{\text{total}} = A_t + A_v = 0.9877 + 0.8112 = 1.7989$$

$$A_{\text{final}}^{(T+V)} = 90.90\%$$

– **Image + Video Fusion**

$$A_{\text{total}} = A_i + A_v = 0.8972 + 0.8112 = 1.7084$$

$$A_{\text{final}}^{(I+V)} = 85.64\%$$

- **Three Modality Present** When all three modalities are available, the final accuracy is the following.
  Step 1: Compute the total score

$$A_{\text{total}} = A_t + A_i + A_v = 0.9877 + 0.8972 + 0.8112 = 2.6961$$

Step 2: Calculate the weights for each modality

$$w_t = \frac{A_t}{A_{\text{total}}} = \frac{0.9877}{2.6961} \approx 0.3663$$
$$w_i = \frac{A_i}{A_{\text{total}}} = \frac{0.8972}{2.6961} \approx 0.3327$$
$$w_v = \frac{A_v}{A_{\text{total}}} = \frac{0.8112}{2.6961} \approx 0.3010$$

Step 3: Compute the final accuracy using weighted aggregation

$$\begin{aligned} A_{\text{final}} &= w_t \cdot A_t + w_i \cdot A_i + w_v \cdot A_v \\ &= (0.3663 \times 0.9877) + (0.3327 \times 0.8972) + (0.3010 \times 0.8112) \\ &\approx 0.3617 + 0.2985 + 0.2443 = 0.9045 \end{aligned}$$

Thus, the final system accuracy is 90.45%.

6.4.2 Using Simple Aggregation

When compared with simple aggregation, the final system accuracy when all three modalities are present would be as shown below.

$$S_{\text{final}} = \frac{98.77 + 89.72 + 81.12}{3} = 89.87\%$$

According to the results shown above, weighted aggregation performs better, showing a more accurate score than the simple aggregation technique.

6.5 Computational Cost and Scalability Analysis

The computational efficiency of the proposed model was examined to assess its practical viability, with each modality exhibiting different computational demands based on the complexity of its feature extraction and fusion processes.

Table 6.2 summarizes the empirical resource usage and theoretical time–space complexities of all three models. The text (BERT-iBiLSTM), image (WaveNet-CNN), and video (HABF) modules exhibit predictable scaling behavior dominated by attention operations, convolutional computations, and hierarchical fusion, respectively. These characteristics confirm that the framework can be deployed efficiently across diverse hardware configurations.

The proposed model uses a modular and sequential architecture, where text, image, and video modalities are processed independently and integrated afterward. This separation allows each module to be deployed on separate compute instances or parallel pipelines, supporting scalability for large-scale review analytics. The system can be deployed on cloud platforms such as AWS or Microsoft Azure using GPU-enabled instances to maintain reliable performance as data volume grows.

Table 6.2: Computational Cost and Complexity of the Proposed Models

Model	Training Time (hours)	Inference Time (sec/input)	GPU Memory (GB)	Time Complexity	Space Complexity
BERT-iBiLSTM (Text)	2.3	0.350	6.2	$O(L^2d)$ L: sequence length, d: embedding dimension	$O(L^2)$
WaveNet-CNN (Image)	4.1	0.580	3.8	$O(WHCK^2F)$ W,H: image size; C: channels; K: kernel; F: filters	$O(WHF)$
HABF (Video)	6.8	2.800	8.5	$O(L^2d)$ L: frames/tokens, d: feature dimension	$O(L^2)$

The proposed integrated SA model introduces a novel framework that unifies the analysis of text, image and video individually or in any combination through a weighted dynamic score-based aggregation in the late fusion stage. In fact, it supersedes traditional unimodal and bimodal approaches by adaptively processing any combination of modalities. The result is a high-level context awareness representation score that is translated into a unified sentiment score and rating so that sentiment can be interpreted in an accurate, comprehensive and holistic way. This particular adaptability makes it highly useful in real industries such as e-Commerce, hospitality and social media analytics, where user feedback is becoming more and more diverse in format and content.

www.ingramcontent.com/pod-product-compliance
Lightning Source LLC
LaVergne TN
LVHW050821061126
851857LV00012B/915